TRANSPORTATION INFRASTRUCTURE –
ROADS, HIGHWAYS, BRIDGES, AIRPORTS AND MASS TRANSIT

RAILROADS IN THE UNITED STATES

CONSIDERATIONS AND DEVELOPMENT PROSPECTS

TRANSPORTATION INFRASTRUCTURE - ROADS, HIGHWAYS, BRIDGES, AIRPORTS AND MASS TRANSIT

Additional books in this series can be found on Nova's website under the Series tab.

Additional E-books in this series can be found on Nova's website under the E-book tab.

TRANSPORTATION INFRASTRUCTURE –
ROADS, HIGHWAYS, BRIDGES, AIRPORTS AND MASS TRANSIT

RAILROADS IN
THE UNITED STATES

CONSIDERATIONS AND
DEVELOPMENT PROSPECTS

CHARLES E. RUSSEL

AND

CAROL M. WOOD

EDITORS

New York

Copyright © 2013 by Nova Science Publishers, Inc.

For permission to use material from this book please contact us:
Telephone 631-231-7269; Fax 631-231-8175
Web Site: http://www.novapublishers.com

NOTICE TO THE READER

Additional color graphics may be available in the e-book version of this book.

Library of Congress Cataloging-in-Publication Data

ISBN: 978-1-62257-727-9

Published by Nova Science Publishers, Inc. † New York

CONTENTS

PREFACE

Efforts to expand rail transportation remain on the radar for policymakers. High speed rail has received attention and its potential continues to be examined. Pressure is building for greater passenger use of freight railroad rights of way. Possible benefits and costs of rail systems are being studied in light of concerns about congestion, emissions and a weaker economy. This book discusses development of rail systems in the United States and the prospects in light of the various benefits and costs to be considered.

Chapter 1 – The provision of $8 billion for intercity passenger rail projects in the 2009 American Recovery and Reinvestment Act (ARRA; P.L. 111-5) reinvigorated efforts to expand intercity passenger rail transportation in the United States. The Obama Administration subsequently announced that it would ask Congress to provide $1 billion annually for high speed rail (HSR) projects. This initiative was reflected in the President's budgets for FY2010 through FY2013. Congress approved $2.5 billion for high speed and intercity passenger rail in FY2010 (P.L. 111-117), but zero in FY2011 (P.L. 112-10) and FY2012 (P.L. 112-55). In addition, the FY2011 appropriations act rescinded $400 million from prior year unobligated balances of program funding.

Chapter 2 – Pressure is building for greater passenger use of freight railroad rights of way. Freight railroad rights of way are owned by private, for-profit corporations, and the routes potentially most useful for passenger service are typically the busiest with freight traffic. In many cases, states or commuter rail authorities have reached agreement with freight railroads to share either their track or right of way. However, unlike Amtrak, which has eminent domain power over freight facilities and can appeal to a federal agency to determine the terms of its access to freight track, other would-be passenger rail operators do not have any statutory leverage when negotiating with freight railroads. This likely increases the price public authorities pay for access and leaves them with no apparent recourse when freight railroads reject their offers.

During House committee mark-up of the Passenger Rail Investment and Improvement Act of 2008 (P.L. 110-432), a provision to require binding arbitration when commuter rail authorities and freight railroads fail to reach agreement over access proved controversial. The committee chose instead to require non-binding arbitration. Some Members of Congress have urged greater reliance on private companies to provide intercity rail services similar to those offered by Amtrak, but such private services may be difficult to develop so long as potential operators lack Amtrak's statutory right to compel freight railroads to carry passenger trains. Freight railroads can be expected to object to such initiatives as unfair "takings" of their private property. In the 112th Congress, the version of surface transportation legislation passed by the Senate (S. 1813) calls for a federal study to evaluate passenger service in shared-use rail corridors and to survey processes for resolving disputes over passenger access.

Passenger access to freight railroad track raises old but recurring questions about the fundamental nature of railroad rights of way. Railroads are not like other businesses that are free to decide how and where they allocate resources solely on the principle of maximizing shareholder returns. While railroad rights of way are private property, more than a century of case law has upheld a public duty on them. The public nature of railroads is evident from the fact that they were designated as "common carriers," granted eminent domain power, and regulated by government. However, the private interest of railroads is protected by the limitation that the government's right to regulate does not mean the right to confiscate. Railroad rights of way, unlike highways, were not considered part of the "public domain." When competition from other modes eroded passenger rail travel, it was confirmed that the public duty attached to railroads could obligate them to operate some trains at a loss, provided the railroad's overall operations were profitable.

The issue for Congress is whether freight railroads and prospective passenger rail authorities should negotiate over the terms of use of railroad property just as any private parties would or if a governmental third party, such as the federal Surface Transportation Board (STB), should have some role in determining the terms. Given that a public service obligation is still attached to railroads, albeit largely lifted with respect to passenger service, do freight railroads have the right to set the price for passenger access unilaterally, or should the public's convenience and necessity be given some consideration? Granting track access rights to potential private operators of passenger service could be a particularly thorny issue. Given the increasing demands on urban rail corridors, Congress might examine alternative methods for managing them. A public "rail port authority" might have some advantages over private railroads in optimizing an urban rail network.

Chapter 3 – Concerns about the weak economy, congestion in the transportation system, and the potentially harmful effects of air emissions generated by the transportation sector have raised awareness of the potential benefits and costs of intercity passenger and freight rail relative to other transportation modes such as highways. GAO was asked to review (1) the extent to which transportation policy tools that provide incentives to shift passenger and freight traffic to rail may generate emissions, congestion, and economic development benefits and (2) how project benefits and costs are assessed for investment in intercity passenger and freight rail and how the strengths and limitations of these assessments impact federal decision making. GAO reviewed studies; interviewed federal, state, local, and other stakeholders regarding methods to assess benefit and cost information; assessed information on project benefits and costs included in rail grant applications; and conducted case studies of selected policies and programs in the United Kingdom and Germany to learn more about their policies designed to provide incentives to shift traffic to rail.

In: Railroads in the United States   ISBN: 978-1-62257-727-9
Editors: Ch. E. Russel and C. M. Wood © 2013 Nova Science Publishers, Inc.

Chapter 1

THE DEVELOPMENT OF HIGH SPEED RAIL IN THE UNITED STATES: ISSUES AND RECENT EVENTS[*]

*David Randall Peterman, John Frittelli
and William J. Mallett*

SUMMARY

The provision of $8 billion for intercity passenger rail projects in the 2009 American Recovery and Reinvestment Act (ARRA; P.L. 111-5) reinvigorated efforts to expand intercity passenger rail transportation in the United States. The Obama Administration subsequently announced that it would ask Congress to provide $1 billion annually for high speed rail (HSR) projects. This initiative was reflected in the President's budgets for FY2010 through FY2013. Congress approved $2.5 billion for high speed and intercity passenger rail in FY2010 (P.L. 111-117), but zero in FY2011 (P.L. 112-10) and FY2012 (P.L. 112-55). In addition, the FY2011 appropriations act rescinded $400 million from prior year unobligated balances of program funding.

---

[*] This is an edited, reformatted and augmented version of the Congressional Research Service Publication, CRS Report for Congress R42337, dated February 1, 2012.

There are two main approaches to building high speed rail (HSR): (1) improving existing tracks and signaling to allow trains to reach speeds of up to 110 miles per hour (mph), generally on track shared with freight trains; and (2) building new tracks dedicated exclusively to high speed passenger rail service, to allow trains to travel at speeds of 200 mph or more. The potential costs, and benefits, are relatively lower with the first approach and higher with the second approach.

Much of the federal funding for HSR to date has focused on improving existing lines in five corridors: Seattle-Portland; Chicago-St. Louis; Chicago-Detroit; the Northeast Corridor (NEC); and Charlotte-Washington, DC. Most of the rest of the money is being used for a largely new system dedicated to passenger trains between San Francisco and Los Angeles, on which speeds could reach up to 220 mph. Plans for HSR in some states were shelved by political leaders opposed to the substantial risks such projects entail, particularly the capital and operating costs; the federal funds allocated to those projects were subsequently redirected to other HSR projects.

Estimates of the cost of constructing HSR vary according to train speed, the topography of the corridor, the cost of right-of-way, and other factors. Few if any HSR lines anywhere in the world have earned enough revenue to cover both their construction and operating costs, even where population density is far greater than anywhere in the United States. Typically, governments have paid the construction costs, and in many cases have subsidized the operating costs as well. These subsidies are often justified by the social benefits ascribed to HSR in relieving congestion, reducing pollution, increasing energy efficiency, and contributing to employment and economic development. It is unclear whether these potential social benefits are commensurate with the likely costs of constructing and operating HSR.

Lack of long-term funding represents a significant obstacle to HSR development in the United States. The federal government does not have a dedicated funding source for HSR, making projects that can take years to build vulnerable to year-to-year changes in discretionary budget allocations.

INTRODUCTION

The provision of $8 billion for intercity passenger rail projects in the 2009 American Recovery and Reinvestment Act (ARRA; P.L. 111-5) reinvigorated the development of high speed intercity passenger rail (HSR) transportation in the United States. While Congress has been interested in HSR since the 1960s, the ARRA funding represented an enormous appropriation in historical terms.[1] The $8 billion was included in ARRA largely at the behest of President Obama, and a subsequent announcement in April 2009 made it clear that the development of HSR is a priority of his Administration.[2] Another $2.5 billion was provided for high speed rail and intercity passenger rail projects in the Transportation, Housing, and Urban Development, and Related Agencies (THUD) Appropriations Act, 2010 (P.L. 111-117). Since then, no additional funding has been appropriated for this program. The FY2011 THUD appropriations act (P.L. 112-10) rescinded $400 million from prior year unobligated balances for high speed and intercity passenger rail projects.

Other than the rescinded amounts, most of the federal HSR funding made available over the past few years has been obligated and various projects are proceeding. In most places, these projects entail upgrading existing lines owned and operated by freight railroads to allow somewhat faster passenger train speeds than are currently possible. On the Chicago-St. Louis line, for example, funding is being used to increase the maximum speed from 79 miles per hour (mph) to 110 mph.[3] Only the HSR project in California is using federal funds for tracks dedicated to passenger trains, on which speeds could reach 220 mph.

Plans for HSR in some states, including Florida, Wisconsin, and Ohio, were shelved by political leaders opposed to the substantial risks such projects entail, particularly the capital and operating costs.[4] Some projects were stopped after federal funds were awarded; these funds were subsequently redirected to HSR projects in other states. Debate on the merits of HSR is likely to continue where projects are ongoing because these projects are often only small steps along the way to providing much faster service in an entire corridor. A key aspect of the debate concerns prospects for the continued development of HSR if no more federal funds are forthcoming.

FEDERAL INITIATIVES TO PROMOTE HIGH SPEED RAIL

Congress has long been interested in the potential benefits of high speed rail. The first high speed rail act, in 1965, contributed to the establishment of the nation's fastest rail service, the Metroliner, on the Washington, DC, to New York City portion of the Northeast Corridor (NEC), when that line was still under private ownership. In the 1970s, ownership of the NEC was transferred from the bankrupt Penn Central to Amtrak, a government-controlled company. At the same time, Congress initiated the Northeast

Corridor Improvement Program, which has funded major infrastructure improvements and, in the late 1990s, purchase of new high speed Acela trains for Amtrak.

Congress has also supported research into various high speed rail technologies and studies of potential high speed corridors outside of the NEC where speeds are currently slower (see **Table 1**). The Federal Railroad Administration (FRA) has calculated that Congress provided a total of $4.17 billion to various high speed rail projects between 1990 and 2007, an average of $232 million annually (not adjusted for inflation).[5] Most of that money went to improvements on the NEC.[6] There have also been state and private sector efforts to develop dedicated high speed rail lines without federal support. But it was only in February 2009, when Congress passed the American Recovery and Reinvestment Act (ARRA; P.L. 111-5), that the federal government dedicated large sums to a national high speed rail program.

Table 1. High Speed Rail Corridors in the United States

Corridor	Length (Miles)	Motive Power	Current Top Speed (mph)	Current Average Speed (mph)
Los Angeles–San Diego, CA	130	Diesel-electric	90	55
Chicago, IL–Detroit/Pontiac, MI	304	Diesel-electric	110	57
New York City–Albany/Schenectady, NY	158	Diesel-electric	110	56
Philadelphia–Harrisburg, PA	104	Electric	110	66
Northeast Corridor (NEC)	454	Electric		
Boston, MA–New York City, NY, segment	229		150	68
New York, NY–Washington, DC, segment	225		135	82

Source: Adapted from Government Accountability Office, *High Speed Passenger Rail*, GAO-09-317. March 2009, Table 1; Average speeds from Appendix II, except Chicago-Detroit, Philadelphia-Harrisburg, and New York City-Albany calculated by CRS based on those corridors' fastest scheduled trips.

Note: The top speeds listed for these corridors are currently attainable only on portions of the routes. For example, on the NEC the top speed of 150 mph is attainable on less than 10% of the total route. The New York-Albany trains rely on electric power while passing through a long tunnel departing New York City.

ARRA provided $8 billion specifically for intercity passenger rail projects, including high speed rail projects. Intercity passenger rail projects were also eligible uses for the $27 billion provided for highways (at the discretion of individual states) and for the $1.5 billion provided for discretionary grants for surface transportation projects "that will have a significant impact on the Nation, a metropolitan area, or a region." Another $90 million was provided for grants to states for intercity passenger rail projects in the FY2009 appropriations act (P.L. 111-8), following a $30 million appropriation for such purposes in the FY2008 appropriations act (P.L. 110-161).

In March 2009, the Obama Administration announced that it would ask Congress to provide $1 billion annually for high speed and intercity passenger rail projects. This initiative was reflected in the President's budgets for FY2010 through FY2013.[7] Congress approved $2.5 billion for high speed rail and intercity passenger rail in FY2010 (P.L. 111-117), but zero in FY2011 (P.L. 112-10) and FY2012 (P.L. 112-55). In addition, the FY2011 appropriations act rescinded $400 million from prior year unobligated balances of program funding.

There have been several other recent congressional initiatives supporting high speed rail (see **Table 2**). The Safe, Accountable, Flexible, Efficient Transportation Equity Act: A Legacy for Users (SAFETEA-LU; P.L. 109-59), as amended by the SAFETEA-LU Technical Corrections Act (P.L. 110-244), made $90 million available for maglev projects.[8] In the fall of 2008, Congress passed the Passenger Rail Investment and Improvement Act of 2008 (Division B of P.L. 110-432). Among other things, this act created a high speed rail development grant program with a total authorization of $1.5 billion over FY2009-FY2013. The act also authorized additional funding for Amtrak to address some of the backlog of maintenance needed to bring the Northeast Corridor up to a state of good repair. It included a provision directing the U.S. Department of Transportation (DOT) to seek private companies to build and operate one or more high speed lines.

In evaluating these efforts, it is important to note that is no single definition of what constitutes high speed rail. The European Union defines HSR as

- separate lines built for speeds of 250 kilometers per hour (kph) (150 mph), or

- existing lines upgraded to speeds of 200 kph (125 mph), or
- upgraded lines whose speeds are constrained by circumstances such as topography or urban development.[9]

Table 2. Recent Congressional Initiatives Related to High Speed Rail Programs created and/or amended in the 109th–112th Congresses

Initiative	Source	Funding	Status
Maglev Deployment Program	Authorized in SAFETEA (§1307, P.L. 109-59) and SAFETEA Technical Corrections Act (P.L. 110-244)	$90 million over FY2008-FY2009. $45 million is for a line from Primm, NV, to Las Vegas; $45 million is for one or more of three eligible projects: the Pittsburgh area, from Baltimore to DC, and from Atlanta to Chattanooga.	Deadline for applications was February 13, 2009. All three eligible projects east of the Mississippi applied for funding. FRA selected the Pittsburgh and Georgia projects to receive funding, in addition to the Nevada project. As of June 2012 the grantees have not used any of the grant funding.
Amtrak Capital Grants	Passenger Rail Investment and Improvement Act of 2008 (PRIIA) (Division B of P.L. 110-432), §101(c)	$5.315 billion authorized over FY2009-FY2013.	$5.1 billion provided for capital grants and debt service FY2009-FY2012, including $1.3 billion provided in ARRA.
NEC High Speed Service Study	PRIIA §212(d)	Not specified.	Amtrak submitted an interim study to Congress on Oct. 21, 2009, and later published two further studies, NEC Master Plan on June 4, 2010, and *A Vision for High-Speed Rail in the Northeast Corridor* on Sept. 27, 2010.
Intercity Passenger Rail Service Corridor Capital Assistance Program	PRIIA §301 (49 USC §24402)	$1.9 billion authorized over FY2009-FY2013.	These three programs were provided a total of $8 billion in ARRA and $2.5 billion in the Consolidated Appropriations Act, 2010. The allocation of that funding among the programs is determined by DOT. No additional funding has been provided since FY2010.
High Speed Rail Corridor Development Program	PRIIA §501 (49 USC §26106)	$1.5 billion authorized over FY2009-FY2013.	
Congestion Grant Program (to alleviate congestion on passenger rail corridors)	PRIIA §302 (49 USC §24105)	$325 million authorized over FY2010-FY2013.	
Capital Assistance to States—Intercity Passenger Rail Service	DOT Appropriations Act, 2008 and 2009	$30 million provided in FY2008; $90 million provided in FY2009.	Funding awarded in several announcements.

Initiative	Source	Funding	Status
Solicitation for new high speed intercity passenger rail system	PRIIA §502	$5 million authorized for planning and preliminary engineering activities for projects selected by DOT.	FRA issued a request for expressions of interest on Dec. 16, 2008. Deadline for response was Sept. 14, 2009. FRA received eight proposals; five were selected for further review. No decision has been announced.
Requirement for implementation of positive train control on main lines where passenger rail service is regularly provided by December 2015	Rail Safety Improvement Act of 2008 (Division A of P.L. 110-432), §104 (49 USC §20157)	$250 million authorized for grants over FY2009-FY2013.	Affected rail operators were required to submit plans for meeting this requirement to FRA by April 2010. FRA reports that all affected railroads are developing implementation plans and are adapting their individual positive train control systems to maximize interoperability.

Source: CRS.

Note: ARRA is the American Recovery and Reinvestment Act of 2009 (P.L. 111-5).

The U.S. government also has several definitions of what constitutes high speed rail. FRA has defined high speed rail as service "that is time-competitive with air and/or auto for travel markets in the approximate range of 100 to 500 miles."[10] As FRA notes, this is a market-driven definition which recognizes that, in choosing a transportation mode, travelers are more interested in total trip time than in top speed, and that travelers evaluate transportation modes not in isolation, but by how those modes compare to each other.

Congress has, at different times, established high speed rail funding programs using different speed-based definitions and eligibility criteria (see **Table 3**).

Table 3. Statutory Definitions of High Speed Rail

Statute	Speed Component of Definition
High Speed Rail Assistance (enacted 1994)	"reasonably expected to reach sustained speeds of more than 125 miles per hour" (49 USC §26105)
High speed rail corridor development program (enacted 2008)	"reasonably expected to reach speeds of at least 110 miles per hour" (49 USC §26106(b)(4))
Railway-highway crossing hazard elimination in high speed rail corridors program (enacted 1991)	"where railroad speeds of 90 miles or more per hour are occurring or can reasonably be expected to occur in the future" (23 USC §104(d)(2)(C)

Source: CRS.

In its strategic plan for high speed rail, FRA defined three categories of high speed rail corridors. These categories differ in terms of top speeds, track characteristics, and service frequency (see **Table 4**). A map of the corridors defined by FRA appears in **Figure 1**.

As these various definitions show, discussions of high speed rail in the United States can refer to trains briefly reaching speeds of 90 mph on tracks shared with freight trains or trains traveling over 200 mph for sustained periods on dedicated track, or both. For clarity, in this chapter the term "higher speed rail" will refer to HSR on shared tracks with speeds up to 150 mph (encompassing both FRA's "Emerging HSR" and "Regional HSR" classifications), and "very high speed rail" will refer to HSR on dedicated tracks with speeds over 150 mph (equivalent to FRA's "Express HSR" classification).

High Speed Rail Project Grants

In response to the $8 billion that Congress provided for high speed and intercity passenger rail capital grants in ARRA, FRA received 45 applications, representing 24 states, requesting a total of approximately $50 billion.[11] Initial funding awards were announced on January 28, 2010, with the biggest awards going to California ($2.25 billion), Florida ($1.25 billion), Illinois ($1.1 billion) and Wisconsin ($810 million). Applications to FRA for the $2.5 billion appropriated in FY2010 numbered 132 and amounted to $8.8 billion. Awards for these funds were initially announced October 28, 2010. California received another $901 million and Florida another $800 million. Iowa received $230 million and Michigan $161 million in this second round of funding.[12]

Table 4. Categories of High Speed Rail in FRA's "Vision for High-Speed Rail in America"

Category	Speed Characteristics
Emerging High Speed Rail	Top speeds of 90-110 mph.
Regional High Speed Rail	Top speeds of 110-150 mph on grade-separated track.
Express High Speed Rail	Top speeds of at least 150 mph on grade-separated track dedicated to passenger service.

Source: Federal Railroad Administration, Vision for High-Speed Rail in America, April 2009, p. 2, http://www.fra.dot.gov/Downloads/Final%20FRA%20HSR%20Strat%20Plan.pdf.

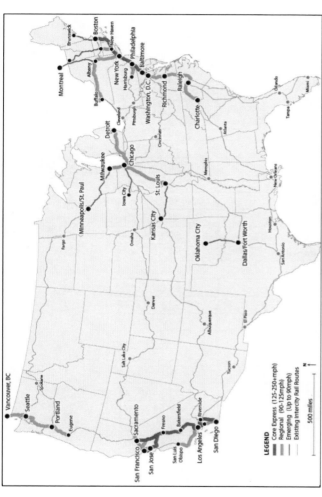

Source: Federal Railroad Administration, High Speed Intercity Passenger Rail Program: Federal Investment Highlights, http://www.fra.dot.gov/rpd/downloads/ HSIPR_Federal_Investment_Highlights_20120203.pdf.

Notes: CRS modified the original map to highlight the different categories of high speed rail service. In this chapter the term "higher speed rail" refers to HSR on shared tracks with speeds up to 150 mph (encompassing both FRA's "Emerging HSR" and "Regional HSR" classifications), and "very high speed rail" refers to HSR on dedicated tracks with speeds over 150 mph (equivalent to FRA's "Express HSR" classification). There are no proposals for Alaska and Hawaii.

Figure1. High Speed Rail Corridors by Proposed Type of Service.

Table 5. High-Speed Intercity Passenger Rail Funding by State

State	Funds Obligated
California	$4,238,197,986
Illinois	$1,905,133,042
Washington	$791,591,702
North Carolina	$546,000,000
New York	$464,422,755
Amtrak (NEC)	$449,944,000
Michigan	$400,732,595
Massachusetts	$105,300,000
Maryland	$91,400,000
Connecticut	$70,000,000
Florida	$66,660,000
Pennsylvania	$66,400,000
Maine	$59,807,836
Vermont	$53,222,258
Missouri	$49,754,545
Minnesota	$45,600,000
Virginia	$44,308,000
Wisconsin	$41,752,955
New Jersey	$38,500,000
Rhode Island	$29,200,000
Texas	$24,067,877
Oregon	$19,496,630
Iowa	$18,709,080
Delaware	$13,750,000
District of Columbia	$7,170,500
Georgia	$4,850,000
Oklahoma	$4,277,843
New Hampshire	$2,240,000
Colorado	$1,400,000
West Virginia	$1,000,000
Nevada	$640,000
Kansas	$337,563
Idaho	$200,000
New Mexico	$100,000

Source: Federal Railroad Administration, HSPIR Project Funding, as of June 20, 2012, http://www.fra.dot.gov/rpd/HSIPR/ProjectFunding.aspx.

Newly elected governors in some states, including Florida, Ohio, and Wisconsin, subsequently decided not to pursue the improvements for which their states had sought federal funds. Florida, for example, dropped plans to build a high speed rail line between Orlando and Tampa. As a result, these federal funds were reallocated to other projects.[13]

According to DOT, nearly 85% of the funding awarded over the past few years is concentrated in six corridors.[14] Investments in five of the corridors are aimed at upgrading existing lines. These five corridors are Seattle-Portland; Chicago-St. Louis; Chicago-Detroit; the Northeast Corridor (NEC); and Charlotte-Washington, DC. In the sixth corridor, Los Angeles-San Francisco, the plans are to build a new very high speed rail line that may allow trains to reach speeds of up to 220 mph. The remaining 15% or so of funding is going toward a multitude of smaller projects throughout the country, including planning studies and station and track improvements. **Table 5** shows obligated funding by state.

As of May 2012, according to FRA, 95% of high speed and intercity passenger rail funding appropriated since FY2009 had been obligated (not including the $400 million rescinded in the FY2011 THUD appropriations bill). However, only about 6% of the total funds had been spent.[15] Progress on two of the largest HSR projects, in the Chicago-St. Louis and Los Angeles-San Francisco corridors, illustrates some of the possibilities and challenges with developing HSR.

Chicago-St. Louis Corridor

Chicago is the center of a number of higher speed rail projects and proposals in the Midwest. This includes improvements to passenger rail service between Chicago and St. Louis. For the most part, the existing 284-mile route between these two cities, which is owned and operated by four different freight railroads, consists of one track with sidings to allow trains to pass. Although the long-term goal is to double-track the entire route and possibly to provide for speeds up to 220 mph,[16] current funding is being used to upgrade much of the existing single track to increase maximum passenger train speeds from 79 mph to 110 mph. Work includes track improvements, new sidings, new signals and warning systems, upgraded stations, and new passenger trains.

Illinois secured $1.1 billion in the initial round of ARRA funding and another $42 million in redirected ARRA funds to improve about 220 miles of the line from St. Louis to Dwight, IL (near Chicago) and to buy new locomotives and rail cars.[17] This is estimated to reduce trip times from 5 hours

30 minutes to between 4 and 5 hours.[18] Illinois later received $186 million in FY2010 intercity passenger rail funding to improve about 40 miles of track between Dwight and Joliet, IL. This is estimated to save another 9 minutes from the overall trip time. By one estimate, building out the whole route for 110 mph will reduce trip times to 3 hours and 50 minutes.[19] Other expected benefits of the project include improved travel time reliability, improved safety, and greater capacity.

Construction work in the Chicago-St. Louis corridor supported with federal funds has been underway since 2010. According to the Illinois Department of Transportation, trains will run at 110 mph on a test segment of the corridor, between Dwight and Pontiac, IL, in 2012.[20] Project completion is scheduled for 2014. Illinois has also received a $1.25 million grant to complete a supplemental Environmental Impact Statement related to double-tracking the corridor.

California High Speed Rail

The California High Speed Rail Authority (CHSRA) is proposing to build a rail line that may allow trains to reach speeds up to 220 mph. In 2008, California voters approved the sale of $9 billion in bonds to partly finance such a system. The Los Angeles to San Francisco line is phase one of a two-phase project, with phase two involving extensions to San Diego and Sacramento. To date, the project has been awarded nearly $4 billion in federal funds. Much of this amount has been obligated to building a segment of phase one between Merced and Bakersfield in California's Central Valley.

Despite the California project's success in attracting federal funds, it remains controversial.[21] Among the main elements of controversy are the project's cost and its financing. In its 2009 business plan CHSRA estimated the cost of building phase one at $36.4 billion in 2010 dollars.[22] In its 2012 draft business plan released on November 1, 2011, the cost of phase one was estimated for two different systems, a full high speed system and a blended system that would make some use of existing passenger rail infrastructure. The full high speed rail system was estimated to cost between $65.4 billion and $74.5 billion and the blended system between $54.9 billion and $66.3 billion (both in 2010 dollars).[23] CHSRA attributed about 80% to 85% of the cost increase since 2009 to the need for additional viaducts, tunnels, embankments, and retaining walls. The other 15% to 20% of the increase results from higher expected construction costs.[24]

The doubling or near doubling of estimated costs for phase one, depending on the proposed system, led to renewed calls for the project to be reexamined or abandoned.[25] Subsequently, a revised business plan, released April 2, 2012, dropped the full high speed rail system scenario as too costly. It provided a revised estimate for the blended system at between \$53.4 billion and \$62.3 billion (in 2011 dollars).[26]

The draft 2012 business plan proposed that nearly two-thirds of the construction funding would come from the federal government, although this share might be somewhat lower depending on the system built, the amount of private sector investment, and other variables.[27] A number of commentators, including California's Legislative Analyst Office (LAO) and the California High-Speed Rail Peer Review Group, have questioned this assumption and have contended that CHSRA's financial plan is highly uncertain.[28] The revised draft business plan continues to rely on the federal government for about two-thirds of the system's funding, but it states that revenue from California's quarterly auctions of greenhouse-gas emissions allowances, beginning November 2012, could be used instead if federal funding is not forthcoming.[29] In response, the LAO has called this plan "very speculative."[30]

Another element of controversy surrounds the choice of the section between Merced and Bakersfield in the Central Valley to be the first segment built. It appears that this section was chosen largely because it may face fewer challenges than other sections in the more heavily populated areas near San Francisco and Los Angeles, increasing the likelihood that California will be able to spend the ARRA money by the statutory deadline of September 30, 2017.[31] Critics, however, claim that this segment of the phase one project will have little utility if the rest of the system is not built.[32] The revised draft business plan commits to building an initial operating segment that connects the Central Valley to the Los Angeles Basin within 10 years.[33]

OPTIONS FOR BUILDING HIGH SPEED RAIL

There are two options for developing high speed rail service; the option chosen determines the level of high speed service that can be attained:

- upgrading existing track, signaling systems, and equipment (e.g., tilting trains) to enable trains to travel somewhat faster over the existing rail network, or
- building new rail lines for the exclusive use of passenger trains enabling trains to travel at much higher speeds than are possible over the existing rail network, which is shared with freight rail.[34]

The advantage of upgrading existing track is its lower cost; one estimate puts the average cost of such upgrades at around $7 million per mile.[35] For example, in the 1990s Amtrak (and commuter railroads[36]) spent around $2 billion—an average of around $9 million per mile, in 2003 dollars— to upgrade the 229-mile north end of the Northeast Corridor (connecting Boston to New York City), including electrifying the route and replacing a bridge.[37] This reduced rail travel time between Boston and New York City from 4 hours to 3 hours and 24 minutes—an increase in average speed over the route from 57 mph to 68 mph. However, track upgrades also have important limitations. One is that many aspects of the rail infrastructure, such as curves and at-grade road crossings, limit the potential speed improvements. Another is that almost all existing track is used for freight trains that operate at slower speeds than passenger trains. Freight traffic may constrain the speed of passenger trains, and FRA regulations limit train speeds on routes that handle both freight and passenger traffic.

Conversely, building new rail lines, including the train, the track, and the signal and communications network, makes much higher speeds possible—up to 200 mph or more. One limitation of that approach is the cost, which is estimated to average $35 million per mile,[38] or more in densely populated areas or difficult terrain. In order to attain such high speeds, freight trains would have to be prohibited from using the track—which also means that freight operators would not be contributing to the construction or maintenance costs. New lines can use either conventional steel wheel on steel rail technology or magnetic levitation (maglev), in which superconducting magnets levitate a train above a guide rail.

Conventional High Speed Rail

With one minor exception, all current high speed rail systems use conventional steel wheel on steel rail technology. At speeds up to around 125 mph, these trains can be pulled by diesel-electric locomotives. For higher speeds, trains powered by externally supplied electricity become necessary. These trains' engines draw power from overhead wires (catenaries). This technology allows for lighter-weight trains, in part because they do not have to carry fuel. Because of their lighter weight, electric trains can stop and start more quickly and produce less wear on the track. These trains can operate at very high speeds: in 2007 a French electric-powered train on conventional tracks reached 357 mph.[39] However, because of the greater costs and diminishing benefits[40] of operating at extremely high speeds, the top operating speed of high speed trains in most countries is around 210 mph.

There are two main reasons why such trains are not widely available in the United States. First, only a small portion of the U.S. rail network is electrified, so most passenger trains must use diesel-electric locomotives.[41] Second, because passenger trains typically use the same tracks as freight trains (and neither generally uses the most advanced collision avoidance systems), federal regulations require that passenger trains have a variety of design features to protect passengers in the event of a train crash. This results in relatively heavy passenger trains, which are thus slower to get up to speed and take longer to stop.

Track

To make very high speed operation possible, rail track must be substantially flat and straight, with shallow curves and gentle changes in elevation. As train speeds increase, the risk of crashes where roads cross the rail line ("at-grade crossings") increases, so safety dictates that high speed tracks not have any at-grade crossings.[42] This is the standard to which new very high speed lines in other countries are usually built. The result is the rail equivalent of the Interstate Highway System, allowing trains to operate at high average speeds without risk from crossing traffic.

A high speed rail system using dedicated track can handle many trains at one time without compromising safety. For example, the Japanese high speed rail network, which began operation in 1964, now has trains running at speeds up to 200 mph, with as little as three minutes of headway (the time separating trains operating on the same track) during peak periods. In almost 50 years of operation, there has never been a fatality due to a train crash on the Japanese high speed network.[43]

Signal and Communications Networks

The prevailing train control system on the U.S. rail network relies on dispatchers at central locations who track the location of trains and signal to train operators when it is safe to proceed onto a stretch of track. This system is somewhat analogous to the air traffic control system, in that the dispatchers can see the location of trains but cannot directly control those trains. Thus, when a train operator does not respond correctly to an operational signal, a collision may occur.

Very high speed rail networks use electronic train control systems (often referred to as "positive train control," or PTC). PTC uses communications systems, global positioning systems, on-board computers with digitized maps, and central control system computers to monitor and control train movements. This technology is intended to improve efficiency and safety through better communication and reducing the threat of human error in the operation of trains. Outside of the NEC, almost none of the nation's rail network is equipped with positive train control. However, the Rail Safety Improvement Act of 2008 requires that rail carriers implement positive train control by December 31, 2015, on main lines over which passengers or poison- or toxic-by-inhalation hazardous materials are transported.[44] This implementation is underway, though there are proposals to extend the deadline to allow more time for implementation.[45]

Magnetic Levitation (Maglev)

Maglev train technology was developed in the United States in the 1960s. It uses electromagnets to suspend (levitate) the train above a guideway, as well as to propel the train. The lack of direct contact (and hence friction) between the train and the guideway allows maglev trains to go very fast. Maglev trains and tracks are expected to experience relatively little wear and tear and hence to have low maintenance costs, although there is not enough experience with maglev in commercial operations to verify this.

Many maglev lines have been proposed, but the few that have been constructed, notably a 19mile line completed in 2004 connecting a Shanghai subway station to Pudong International Airport, have been relatively short. As a consequence, the costs of constructing and maintaining an intercity maglev line are unclear. It is generally believed that such projects are very expensive, in part because the need for a relatively straight guideway may require costly land acquisition and tunneling. Japan and Germany have operated maglev test tracks since the 1970s and 1980s, respectively, but neither country has gone on to build the commercial maglev lines that were envisioned. Congress established a program to promote maglev in the United States in the 1990s, but none of the projects that received federal support have advanced beyond the planning stage.

Because conventional train technology is capable of speeds comparable to maglev technology, and the costs of maglev implementation are probably very high, there is little impetus to adopt maglev technology. Moreover, maglev trains could not operate over the existing rail network, but would require an entirely separate network. China reportedly built the Shanghai line in part to examine maglev technology as a candidate for high speed lines it planned; it subsequently chose conventional train technology for its high speed rail network.

The Central Japan Railway Company (JR Central) has announced that it will deal with capacity limitations on its high speed line between Tokyo and Osaka, the most heavily traveled intercity rail segment in the world, by building a maglev line roughly parallel to the existing line. The planned train would travel at 300 mph over the 175 miles between Tokyo and Nagoya and would eventually be extended to Osaka. Due in part to the geographic constraints—as the line would pass through mountainous areas, as well as densely populated areas, about 80% of the track would be located on viaducts or in tunnels—JR Central has estimated the cost of building the Tokyo-Nagoya segment at 5.1 trillion yen (around $60 billion), or a little less than $350 million per mile.[46] The full line is estimated to cost 9 trillion yen (about $110 billion).[47] Although the Japanese government has approved the project it is not certain that the line will be built; estimated costs have risen, and the need is unclear given Japan's population decline.

COST ISSUES

The costs of HSR can be divided into two general categories: infrastructure costs, including the costs of building the line and maintaining it, and operating costs, such as labor and fuel, which tend to vary according to the amount of train service offered. Of the many high speed routes in the world, it is thought that only two have earned enough revenue to cover both their infrastructure and operating costs.[48]

Infrastructure Costs

High speed rail requires a significant up-front capital outlay for development of the fixed infrastructure (right-of-way, track, signals, and stations) and for its upkeep. However, system costs are highly site- and project-specific. A leading determinant of cost is whether a new right-of-way is planned or if an existing railroad right-of-way is going to be improved. Another key cost determinant is speed. Generally, as speed increases, the cost of providing the infrastructure to attain that speed rises at an increasing rate. The highest speeds will require grade-separated corridors, limited curvature, and modest gradients so that passengers do not experience extreme discomfort at high speeds. As speed increases, the signaling and communications system must be more advanced (and costly) to ensure safe operations. Building a route through mountainous terrain is more costly than construction on level terrain, and building a route through an urban area is generally costlier than construction in a rural area.

These drivers of cost are evident in the various projects to build higher speed or very high speed rail in the United States. For instance, a proposed route between Los Angeles (Anaheim) and Las Vegas would utilize maglev technology, with a top speed of 311 mph, at an estimated cost of nearly $12 billion, or $48 million per route mile. A proposed alternative would use conventional steel rail, with a top speed of 150 mph, and, rather than beginning in Anaheim, would start in Victorville, CA, which is beyond the mountains to the north of Los Angeles. The estimated cost of this alternative is nearly $4 billion or $22 million per route mile. Much of the decrease in estimated cost is due to not bringing the line through the mountains into the Los Angeles area, which in turn may lower its attractiveness to potential riders.[49]

In contrast to these projects involving acquisition of new rights-of-way, a project to increase train speeds between Chicago and other Midwest cities would involve improvements to approximately 3,000 miles of existing track at an estimated cost of $7.7 billion, or about $2.5 million per route mile. A Government Accountability Office (GAO) review of six projects involving incremental track improvements found that per-mile costs ranged from $4.1 million to $11.4 million.[50] The DOT Inspector General has estimated that reducing travel time between Washington, DC, and New York City and between New York City and Boston by a half hour would require corridor improvements totaling $14 billion (or about $31 million per route mile).[51]

Since the objective of building or improving a rail line is passenger mobility, rail project costs could be compared with the costs of alternative methods of increasing mobility, such as expanding a highway or an airport. The cost of highway or airport expansion is also highly project- and site-specific. Comparing costs on a per-mile basis is not as useful as comparing costs on a per passenger-mile basis (the cost of moving one passenger one mile) or comparing the reductions in total travel time across alternative modal projects. These measures incorporate the improvement in passenger throughput expected from the construction project. However, comparing costs and benefits of modal options in this manner is not common because of institutional and organizational obstacles.[52] These include a federal DOT that is organized by modal segments, congressional authorizing committees organized by mode, earmarking of projects, prohibitions in state trust fund and federal trust fund financing, and industry advocacy that is largely organized by mode.[53]

In addition, there is evidence that transportation project costs are routinely underestimated. One study examined 258 transportation infrastructure projects around the world and found that in almost 90% of the cases costs were underestimated, that actual costs on average were 28% higher than estimated, and that rail projects in particular were the most severely underestimated, costing on average 45% more than estimated.[54]

Most U.S. railroad track is owned and maintained by private freight railroad companies whose trains operate more economically at slower speeds. Improving the quality of this track to allow for higher speed passenger trains could involve rebuilding track substructure, such as replacing the ballast, improving drainage, or replacing wood ties with concrete ties, as well as upgrading signaling and communications systems. Although the host freight railroads might gain some benefit from such improvements, they may be reluctant to fund them, as they may gain little advantage from being able to operate freight trains at higher speeds.

More importantly, because intercity passenger and freight trains, as well as commuter trains, share the track in many corridors where higher speed service is proposed, it will be necessary to increase capacity on these routes to avoid delays caused by interference from other trains. For example, Amtrak's on-time performance on the NEC,[55] which has multiple tracks and on which Amtrak controls the dispatching, was around 83% in FY2011, but its on-time performance outside the NEC,[56] where there is often only a single track and where dispatching is controlled by freight rail companies, was 78% for short-distance trains and 64% for long distance trains.[57] According to Amtrak, many delays are due to interference from freight trains, and to a lesser extent, commuter trains. The simplest way to increase capacity is to add sidings to allow slower trains make way for faster trains to pass, but significant improvements in speed and reliability may require installing a second track with high-speed crossovers so trains can shift from one track to the other, a layout which more than doubles route capacity.[58]

Operating Costs and Revenues

Once a higher speed or very high speed infrastructure has been completed, operating costs can be a significant public expense if the train operator cannot generate sufficient revenue from passenger fares. Operating costs include labor, fuel or electric power, equipment and track maintenance, track access charges, and other costs that vary depending on the number of trains that are operated. In the United States, all intercity passenger operations except Amtrak's Acela service are subsidized, in the sense that federal and state governments supplement revenues from ticket sales, as these are insufficient to cover the costs of operating the trains plus a portion of general administrative expenses. Few if any passenger rail operations anywhere in the world generate sufficient revenue to cover all capital as well as operating costs.

Some high-speed rail project sponsors have estimated that their services would be able to operate without public subsidies once construction is complete. Additionally, some supporters of high speed rail projects have asserted that profit-maximizing private companies could operate rail services without subsidy, especially in corridors where air and highway congestion are extreme.

The organizational structure of passenger rail is not conducive to a market environment in which competition among carriers exerts downward pressure on operating costs. The "low-cost carrier" phenomenon in the airline and intercity bus industries, in which multiple carriers compete with one another over the same infrastructure, is not practicable in the passenger rail industry.

Airlines and bus lines operate using publicly owned infrastructure to which all carriers have access on similar terms. Most track suitable for passenger service in the United States, on the other hand, is controlled by railroads whose main business is operating freight trains rather than accommodating passenger operations. Indeed, under federal law freight railroads are not obligated to carry trains of passenger operators other than Amtrak.[59] The freight railroads have little incentive to negotiate access charges favorable to potential passenger operators, especially where their trains would interfere with freight operations or would necessitate a higher level of track maintenance. This poses a considerable obstacle to state governments or private companies seeking to operate high-speed passenger trains in competition with Amtrak or on routes Amtrak does not serve.[60]

Operating costs aside, the other key determinant of whether high speed rail can be profitable without subsidies is fare revenue, which is dependent on ridership levels and how much riders would be willing to pay for the service.[61]

The cost-effectiveness of higher speed and very high speed rail depends on achieving high ridership levels. Estimates of the level of ridership needed to justify the cost of a high speed line similar to those in other countries range from 6 million to 9 million riders in the first year.[62] To put that figure in context, Amtrak's current high speed service, the Acela, which began operating in 2000 in the most densely populated corridor in the United States, carried 3.4 million passengers in FY2011.[63]

Ridership, of course, will depend heavily on the fares charged. Most plans for very high speed systems are premised on their ability to attract business customers who currently travel by air, as these are the travelers most willing to pay high fares for premium service. Despite an airplane's speed advantage, HSR can be time-competitive with an airplane if distances between cities are less than about 400-500 miles, given that security screening and pre-boarding wait times generally are significantly longer for air travelers than they are for train riders. Amtrak has been competitive with the airlines between certain cities along the Northeast Corridor. It captures 69% of the air/rail market share between Washington, DC, and New York City and 51% of the air/rail market share between New York City and Boston.[64] However, Amtrak only captures about 5% of the air/rail market share for trips from Washington, DC, to Boston, a distance of about 440 miles, which takes nearly seven hours even on the Acela.

It is more difficult for rail to compete with automobile transportation. If a traveler needs to make multiple stops en route to or around the destination city, a car may be more convenient, especially if the destination city lacks an extensive mass transit system. Driving is likely to be less expensive than rail if two or more people are traveling together, since the added cost of each additional traveler is virtually zero for passenger cars, and if tolls and parking fees are low. People traveling for leisure or personal reasons are likely to be more price-sensitive than business travelers, and their willingness to use the train instead of a personal car may depend in good part on the availability of low-cost fares.

High speed trains are not expected to compete well against intercity buses in many instances because bus travelers are more concerned about price than about travel time or comfort. Recent improvements in intercity bus service quality and frequency may reduce demand for high speed rail in some markets.

Trains depend on population density to operate efficiently. To compete with the airlines, trains must depart frequently but they also must fill a large proportion of their seats to generate sufficient ticket revenue if they hope to cover their operating costs. Not only is the population size of a city important but also the concentration of economic activity in the central business district or otherwise near the train station(s). Although the nation as a whole is becoming more urbanized, trends show that employment is steadily decentralizing in almost all U.S. cities, which may raise questions about the viability of high speed rail as a transportation alternative for many business travelers.[65] It is worth noting that tickets to or from New York City accounted for nearly 30% of Amtrak's total ridership in 2010.[66] New York has an extremely high population density, has a large concentration of businesses within walking distance of the train station, and is the only city in the country where more residents (55%) do not own an automobile than do.[67]

POTENTIAL BENEFITS OF HIGH SPEED PASSENGER RAIL

With decades of experience from around the world, conventional HSR can be considered a proven technology that potentially offers a convenient and comfortable way to travel between major urban centers. However, HSR has come in for criticism based on concerns about its cost-effectiveness compared to travel by air or highway. Assessments of cost-effectiveness are likely to depend, in part, on the ability of HSR to provide various social goods whose benefits will not be reflected in passenger revenues.

Alleviating Highway and Airport Congestion

In heavily traveled and congested corridors, HSR has the potential to relieve highway and air traffic congestion, and thereby to reduce the need to pay for capacity expansions of roads and airports.[68]

With respect to highway congestion relief, many studies estimate that HSR will have little positive effect because most highway traffic is local and the diversion of intercity trips from highway to rail will be small. In a 1997 study, FRA estimated that in most cases rail improvements would divert only 3%-6% of intercity automobile trips, and even less in corridors with average trip lengths under 150 miles.[69] DOT's Inspector General (IG) found much the same thing in a more recent analysis of HSR in the Northeast Corridor, estimating that reductions of one hour in rail trip times from Boston to New York and from New York to Washington would reduce automobile ridership along the NEC by less than 1%.[70] Planners of a high speed rail link in Florida between Orlando and Tampa, a distance of about 84 miles, estimated that it would shift 11% of those driving between the two cities to the train, but because most of the traffic on the main highway linking the two cities, Interstate 4, is not travelling between Orlando and Tampa, the HSR project was estimated to reduce traffic on the busiest sections of I-4 by less than 2%.[71]

Since HSR is more comparable to commercial air travel than to automobile travel, it is likely that in the right circumstances a significant share of air travelers would switch to HSR. The IG's study of the NEC estimated that 11%-20% would divert to HSR from air, depending upon train speeds, concluding that "this would provide congestion relief at NEC airports and in NEC airspace."[72]

Such high diversion rates would not necessarily reduce airport congestion. Airlines might substitute smaller aircraft for larger ones, or replace flights to locations accessible by rail with flights to and from other locations. The net effects of such changes may be positive, as they may improve intercity transport links overall. However, it is possible that a smaller airport in a community served by HSR could suffer a disproportionate loss of its air service.[73] Even in heavily congested areas, HSR may be a more costly way of relieving air traffic congestion on a per-passenger basis than some combination of measures such as expanding airport capacity, applying congestion pricing to takeoff and landing slots, and implementing an enhanced air traffic control system.[74]

Alleviating Pollution and Reducing Energy Consumption

Another major benefit claimed for HSR is that it uses less energy and is relatively less polluting than other modes of intercity transportation.[75] While the physics of rail do generally provide favorable energy intensity and carbon emission attributes in comparison with highway and air travel, such claims tend to rest heavily on assumed high passenger loads and the use of clean sources of electricity generation to power the trains. Moreover, they tend to ignore the energy and carbon emission of building, maintaining, and rebuilding the infrastructure that supports each mode, and they tend to assume automotive and airplane engine technology will not become more energy efficient in the future.

Completed as part of a wide-ranging review of transportation policy in the United Kingdom, an analysis of building a high speed rail system connecting

London with Glasgow and Edinburgh (distances of approximately 350 miles and 330 miles, respectively), including its energy use and carbon emissions profile, concluded:

> high level analysis of the potential carbon benefits from modal shift from air to high speed rail suggests that these benefits would be small relative to the very high cost of constructing and operating such a scheme, and that under current assumptions a high speed line connecting London to Scotland is unlikely to be a cost-effective policy for achieving reductions in carbon emissions compared to other policy measures.[76]

Because HSR will only capture a relatively small share of total passenger trips, it is also unlikely to make much difference in achieving greenhouse gas reduction targets and in reducing petroleum consumption. A study of the potential benefits of HSR in Sweden concluded that investment in rail networks is a less cost-effective climate policy instrument than general policies, such as increased fuel taxes.[77] Similarly, analysis of a proposed line from London to Scotland estimated carbon savings would be 0.2% of the UK's current emissions, assuming that all flyers take the train and HSR emits no greenhouse gases.[78]

Promoting Economic Development

There is no doubt that HSR projects create employment in planning, design, and construction. Research shows that infrastructure spending tends to create more jobs than other types of spending.[79] The California High Speed Rail Authority (CHSRA) claims that its planned HSR system will create 100,000 construction-related jobs each year during the building phase.[80]

The longer-term impact of HSR in spurring economic development and encouraging potentially beneficial changes in land use around high speed rail stations, by contrast, is disputed. CHSRA claims that high speed rail in California will create 450,000 permanent jobs due to faster economic growth.[81] Looking at the experience of HSR in Japan, one study argues "the claims that a multiplier effect (or economic development effect) of 450,000 jobs as a result of the introduction of CHSR [California HSR] are not likely to be realized."[82] Moreover, GAO pointed out in 2009 that "while benefits such as improvements in economic development and employment may represent real benefits for the jurisdiction in which a new high speed rail service is located, from another jurisdiction's perspective or from a national view they may represent a transfer or relocation of benefits."[83] On the question of whether HSR can provide broader economic benefits by allowing workers greater access to jobs and improving business travel, the UK study discussed earlier found that "such effects are quite limited in mature economies with well developed infrastructure."[84]

Improving Transportation Safety

HSR in other countries generally has a very good safety record. France's TGV, for example, boasts that it has never had a single on-board fatality running at high speed in over two decades of operation. However, it is unlikely that HSR will significantly reduce the number of transportation-related deaths and injuries in the United States. Autos are by far the most dangerous form of passenger travel, in terms of fatalities per passenger-mile, and, as noted above, the ability of HSR to divert highway travelers to rail is likely to be limited. The diversion of flyers to trains would make little difference in terms of passenger safety because air transportation is also very safe.

Providing Travelers a Choice of Modes

There is some value in providing travelers with a choice of modes, particularly for those unable or unwilling to fly or drive. In congested corridors, frequent and reliable HSR could provide travelers an attractive alternative to dealing with the frustrations of traffic bottlenecks and airline delays. Intercity rail can also be a relatively comfortable way to travel, affording travelers more seating room than airplanes or buses and greater opportunity to walk around. However, while these benefits accrue to individual users of HSR, it is not apparent that greater comfort and convenience bring social benefits that would justify public subsidies.

Making the Transportation System More Reliable

Many different types of events can dramatically disrupt a transportation system. These include floods, snowstorms, hurricanes, earthquakes, fires, and terrorism. During such events, it can be very valuable to have extra capacity to handle extra demand or an alternative means of travel when other means fail.

For example, rail service often continues when bad weather grounds air service.[85] Building in redundancy to any system entails added costs, but the availability of alternatives tends to make the system as a whole more reliable during unusual events and emergencies.[86]

HIGH SPEED RAIL FUNDING CONSIDERATIONS

The demand for HSR funding is potentially very great. There are many potential projects, and if currently funded projects result in significantly increased train usage, additional projects are likely to be put forward. For example, work now underway to improve service between Chicago and St. Louis may be followed by proposals to double-track the existing line at additional cost, and there have been studies for a future 220 mph line between the two cities at an estimated cost of $12.6 billion (in 2012 dollars).[87] As noted earlier, the most recent cost estimate for Phase 1 of the California HSR is now itself around $60 billion.

In 2009, the House Transportation and Infrastructure (T&I) Committee's proposal for surface transportation authorization included $50 billion over six years for high speed rail development, an average of $8.3 billion annually.[88] However, the House T&I proposal for high speed rail did not include a dedicated revenue source. Given that HSR projects can require 10 years or more to develop, funding projects in the face of changing political priorities will be difficult without a dedicated funding source.[89] Otherwise, rail projects must compete with the programs for limited discretionary funding. Only about $15 billion of DOT's funding came from the general fund in FY2012, with the balance coming from motor fuel taxes dedicated to the highway trust fund. Providing another $1 billion in general fund money for high speed rail each year, let alone $8.3 billion, would require a significant increase in DOT's General Fund appropriation.

Several options have been advanced to fund an intercity passenger rail development program:

- Dedicating a portion of the highway trust fund's revenues. This approach is not promising, as the highway trust fund's outlays to highway and transit currently exceed its revenues.
- Adding a tax onto the tickets of intercity rail passengers, just as the Airport and Airway Trust Fund is funded in part by a tax on airline tickets. In addition to raising the price of the rail travel it is meant to

support, this proposal would produce relatively small amounts of revenue: a 10% tax on Amtrak tickets in FY2011 would have raised $189 million, assuming that ridership would not have declined as a result of the price increase.

- Dedicating a portion of the revenues from proposed greenhouse gas emissions reduction programs to a rail trust fund. To date, however, Congress has not established greenhouse gas control programs that would raise significant sums.

- Using bonds, including tax-exempt bonds and tax-credit bonds, to fund development of high speed rail lines. Based on the revenue experience of high speed lines in other countries, it appears likely that the bonds would have to be repaid primarily by the federal or state governments, or both.

- Obtaining funding from the private sector. The United States has not seen private investment in passenger rail infrastructure in many decades; the most notable proposal now pending, for a privately owned line between Victorville, CA and Las Vegas is dependent upon a $4.9 billion federal loan, meaning that taxpayers could be at risk if the project fails to generate sufficient revenue.[90]

HIGH SPEED RAIL IN OTHER COUNTRIES

Proponents of HSR often cite the networks in Japan, France, and other countries, with the implication that their adoption of HSR demonstrates the feasibility and desirability of building HSR lines in the United States. This conclusion may not be warranted. The motives that led other countries to implement very high speed rail lines are varied. Some, like Japan and China, did so originally in part to meet the demand on already overcrowded conventional rail lines. Others did so to promote economic development in certain locations or encourage rail travel in the face of the growing role of car and air travel.

In Europe and Japan, HSR has succeeded in capturing market share from commercial aviation. For example, rail has captured 85% of the air/rail market between Tokyo and Osaka (a distance of 320 miles, with a fastest scheduled

rail travel time of 2 hours 25 minutes), and 74% of the air/rail market between Rome and Bologna (a distance of 222 miles, with a fastest schedule rail travel time of 2 hours 44 minutes).[91]

The relative efficiency of HSR as a transportation investment varies among countries, depending upon the interplay of many factors, including geography, economics, and government policies. For example, compared to the United States, countries with HSR have higher population densities, smaller land areas, lower per capita levels of car ownership, higher gasoline prices, lower levels of car use (measured both by number of trips per day and average distance per trip), and higher levels of public transportation availability and use.

Also, there is a significant difference in the structure of the rail industry in countries with HSR compared to the United States. In most of those countries, high speed rail was implemented by state-owned or state-supported rail infrastructure companies and is operated by state-owned rail companies whose principal business is passenger, rather than freight, transportation. By contrast, in the United States the rail network is almost entirely owned by private companies specializing in freight transportation.

The history of HSR development in other countries reveals a recurring tension between economic analysis and political pressure in HSR development. A country's initial HSR line is usually built in a location where the investment makes the most sense economically, in terms of population density and travel demand. Once that line is built, and if it is considered successful, the desire for similar benefits in other parts of the country can result in political pressure to build additional lines, even if economic analysis indicates that these are unlikely to be as successful as the initial line. Japan is perhaps the best example, in part because it has been building HSR lines for the longest time: its first HSR line was the most successful the world has seen, but subsequent lines have carried fewer passengers and had weaker financial performance.

For more information on the development of HSR in other countries see the **Appendix**.

CONSIDERATIONS FOR CONGRESS

In considering further initiatives regarding HSR, there are a number of issues Congress may wish to examine. The first of these is the rationale for building HSR. Proponents of HSR contend that it provides a number of direct and indirect benefits to travelers and the general public, some of which may not be apparent until far into the future. The extent of those benefits would depend largely on the level of ridership, which is difficult to forecast accurately and is likely to be influenced by the adoption or rejection of policies that would encourage people to use high speed rail. Other countries with high speed rail systems support HSR use through both incentives (e.g., widespread provision of a complementary mode, public transit) and disincentives (e.g., high road tolls and high taxes on motor fuel to make automobile use more expensive). Without similar policies in place, HSR ridership in the United States may not fulfill expectations based on the experiences of other countries.

Many of the benefits ascribed to HSR, such as improved mobility, reductions in imported energy, reduced greenhouse gas emissions, and so forth, would come from very high speed rail lines. Yet very high speed lines are expensive and potentially risky investments. Very high speed rail competes primarily with commercial aviation, which receives relatively little support from general Treasury funds compared to the level of funding which would likely be required to develop and operate a high speed rail network. And while very high speed rail might help to relieve airport congestion, Congress is supporting improvements which are expected to significantly expand the aviation system's capacity.

Should Congress decide to continue federal support for HSR, it would need to address a number of issues related to program financing:

- Should overall transportation funding be increased to include funding for HSR, or should some funding from existing highway and transit programs be redirected to HSR? The Obama Administration's FY2013 budget proposed $1 billion for what it calls "high-speed rail implementation."[92]
- What is the desirable allocation of the costs of high speed rail development among federal, state, and local governments and the private sector? Congress specified that the $8 billion provided in ARRA would be provided without requiring any local matching funds, but the HSR development program authorized in the Passenger Rail Investment and Improvement Act of 2008 (PRIIA) provided that the federal share of grants under that program should not exceed 80%. Most highway construction receives an 80% federal match, but the federal share of most rail transit projects is less.[93]
- How should federal funds be allocated among types of HSR? One or two successful very HSR projects might demonstrate HSR's potential and build public support, but they could also consume large amounts of funding. Incremental improvements to passenger routes in many

parts of the country might bring better rail service to more people, but would probably not achieve the high density, very high speed operations generally associated with the concept of HSR.

- Which HSR projects should receive funding? In the HSR development program, Congress required that projects be part of a state rail plan or the national rail plan in order to receive funding. The FRA is currently developing a national rail plan,[94] but high speed rail development grants have been awarded prior to the completion of the plan. The basis FRA has used for selecting projects to be funded is not always clear. Nor is it clear whether FRA's national rail plan will reflect the rail plans of the states or will lay out a national rail vision that may not coincide with individual states' priorities.

Beyond the development costs, Congress may wish to consider how to pay for maintaining and operating an HSR system over the long term. Passenger revenues may not be sufficient to cover the operating costs of high speed lines, including the maintenance of the new HSR infrastructure. The federal government has not assumed long-term responsibility for infrastructure, other than that owned by Amtrak, and has not supported train operations other than those deemed to be part of Amtrak's national network. Measures to ensure adequate funding for train operations and infrastructure maintenance may be desirable to protect the federal investment in HSR.

APPENDIX. EXPERIENCE WITH HSR IN OTHER COUNTRIES

Following are brief accounts of high speed rail networks in selected countries. Except where otherwise indicated, these countries have lines currently operating at speeds of 186 mph or more.

Japan

Japan may be the ideal country, geographically, for high speed rail; its main island is relatively long and narrow, so that its relatively large population is concentrated in cities arrayed along a corridor. Japan opened its first high speed rail line, between Tokyo and Osaka, in 1964.[95] That line was built to expand capacity in an overcrowded rail corridor. From its inception it earned enough revenue to cover its operating costs, and reportedly earned enough money within its first few years to pay back its construction costs. The success of the Tokyo-Osaka line encouraged expansion, and the Japanese government has supported construction of other high speed lines. As of 2011, the high speed rail network was 1,665 miles in length, with more under construction.[96] Currently, new lines are funded by public-private partnerships, with part of the funding coming from the now-privatized regional rail companies, and the rest from the national and local governments.

Since 1987, when the government began the privatization of Japan National Railways, all high speed lines have been operated by private companies. Current information on the profitability of individual high speed lines is not available, but all of the more recent lines have much lower ridership than the heavily traveled Tokyo-Osaka line.

France

France opened its first high speed rail line in 1981, between Paris and Lyon. Its high speed trains are referred to as TGVs (*Trains à Grande Vitesse*). As of 2011, the system has approximately 1,185 miles of high speed rail line, with more under construction.[97] Because of the relatively low population density of France and the central role of Paris (the nation's capital and largest population center), the French high speed rail network has been developed as spokes radiating outward from Paris. Regional governments are responsible for a significant share of construction costs. The state-owned rail operating company, SNCF, reports that its TGVs have taken the dominant share of the air-rail travel market in several of the high speed corridors, taking over 90% in the Paris-Lyon market (with a TGV travel time of less than two hours) and about 60% in corridors where the TGV travel time is around three hours.[98]

Germany

Article 87 of the German Constitution makes rail transport a government responsibility.[99] Germany opened its first high speed rail line in 1991. Its high speed trains are called InterCityExpress (ICE).

Germany's network varies significantly from that of its neighbor, France. Due in part to the more geographically distributed political demands of a federal system of government and in part to a denser and more evenly distributed population, Germany's high speed rail service has been developed to connect many hubs rather than centering on a single city. Germany's high speed trains also have more stops than those of France, whose system emphasizes connecting distant city pairs with few intermediate stops. These considerations have led Germany to put more emphasis on upgrading existing rail lines to accommodate higher speed service, and less emphasis on building entirely new high speed lines. One result is that Germany's high speed trains have longer average trip times than do those of France over comparable distances.

Spain

Spain opened its first high speed rail line in 1992. Like France, its population density is relatively low by European standards, and, except for Madrid, the capital and largest city, which is located in the center of the country, the population is largely concentrated near the coasts. Spain's conventional rail network was built using a wider gauge (i.e., the distance between the two parallel rails) than the international standard. Its high speed rail network is being built to the international standard, producing two separate rail networks. Many trains have special equipment to allow them to operate on both networks.

Government spending on rail infrastructure (both high speed and conventional) surpassed spending on roads in 2003. The Spanish government's Ministry of Public Works has a Strategic Plan for Infrastructure and Transport for the period 2005-2020.[100] The largest portion of the spending in the Plan— €109 billion (44% of the total)—is for railways, primarily for increasing the size of the high speed rail network to 6,200 miles by the year 2020, and putting 90% of the population within 30 miles of a station.[101] The high speed rail network is seen as a way of improving mobility with less environmental impact than automobile or air travel, and as a way of promoting the development of Spain's regions, as well as creating transportation-related employment.

China

China is developing an extensive high speed rail system in part to relieve the pressure of both passenger and freight demand on its overcrowded existing rail system,[102] in part to improve transportation connections between its different regions, and in part to promote the economy of less developed regions. China is upgrading parts of its existing rail network to achieve speeds of 120-150 mph, and is building new dedicated electrified lines to enable speeds of 180 mph or more. The national government has announced plans to have approximately 10,000 miles of high speed lines (including both upgraded existing lines and new dedicated electrified lines) in operation by 2020.[103] China accelerated its HSR construction schedule in 2008-2010, in part to stimulate the economy. But in the wake of a high-profile collision between two high-speed trains that killed 40 people in the summer of 2011, China has acknowledged that it expanded the network too quickly, and has slowed the pace of its HSR construction.[104]

Taiwan

Taiwan is an island nation slightly smaller than Maryland and Delaware combined, with a population estimated at around 23 million people, most of whom live on the western side of the island. The high speed line runs 214 miles north to south along the western side of the country. Upon its completion in 2007, it cut end-to-end travel times from 4.5 hours to 90 minutes.[105]

The Taiwanese government executed a build-operate-transfer contract with a private consortium, the Taiwan High Speed Rail Corporation, to develop the line at a cost of approximately $15 billion. Some 87% of the line had to be placed either in tunnels or on viaducts.[106] Initial ridership projections were around 65 million passengers annually, based in part on domestic airline ridership, which had doubled from 9 million passengers in 1992 to 18 million in 1997. However, subsequent economic difficulties resulted in airline ridership dropping to 9 million in 2005, and the opening of a new highway also increased the attractiveness of highway travel.[107] In 2011, rail ridership totaled 41.6 million passengers.[108] In 2009, the Taiwanese government took control of the Taiwan High Speed Rail Corporation, which was on the brink of bankruptcy.[109] Reportedly, reductions in the interest rates on the corporation's debt (thanks to government guarantees) combined with increasing ridership resulted in a profit in 2011.[110]

South Korea

The Republic of Korea is slightly larger in area than the state of Indiana, with a population estimated at 49 million people. Korea began construction of a 255-mile high speed line in 1992, connecting its capital, Seoul (population 10 million), with its main port, Busan (population 3 million). This corridor serves 70% of the nation's population, and was previously serviced by a conventional line. The project was substantially completed in 2010, with a small amount of new track in central cities yet to be built. End-to-end travel time was cut from 4 hours to around 2 hours and 20 minutes, and ridership was reported to be 140,000 passengers a day in 2011 (about 51 million passengers, annually).[111] Initial cost estimates were around $5 billion, but the ultimate project cost was around $20 billion.[112] The project was costly in part due to the challenging terrain; nearly half of the line is in tunnels and another quarter on viaducts, with only a quarter at grade.[113]

End Notes

[1] As one observer has noted, "it is impossible to overstate how big a sea change this represents ... [the] $8 billion is seventeen times as much money as Congress has provided for these programs over the past 10 fiscal years." *Transportation Weekly*, "President to Sign Stimulus Bill Today," February 17, 2009, p. 5.

[2] At the April announcement, the President released a strategic plan for HSR, including a proposal for budgeting an additional $1 billion a year for five years. The plan identifies the funding as "a down payment to jump-start a potential world-class passenger rail system and sets the direction of transportation policy for the future." U.S. Department of Transportation, "President Obama, Vice President Biden, Secretary LaHood Call for U.S. High-Speed Passenger Trains," Press Release, Thursday April 16, 2009, DOT 51-09, http:// www.fra.dot.gov/Downloads/RRdev/ hsrpressrelease.pdf.

[3] Improvements on the Northeast Corridor between Washington and Boston will increase speeds on some stretches from 135 mph to 160 mph. See Department of Transportation, "Transportation U.S. Transportation Secretary LaHood Announces $2 Billion for High-Speed Intercity Rail Projects to Grow Jobs, Boost U.S. Manufacturing and Transform Travel in America," Press Release DOT 57-11, May 9, 2011, http://www.fra.dot.gov/roa/ press_releases/fp_DOT_5711.shtml.

[4] Timothy Williams, "Florida's Governor Rejects High-Speed Rail Line, Fearing Cost to Taxpayers," *New York Times*, February 16, 2011, http://www.nytimes.com/2011/02/17/us/ 17rail.html.

[5] E-mail from Neil Moyer, Chief, Intercity Passenger Rail Analysis Division, FRA, February 1, 2008.

[6] U.S. Government Accountability Office, *High Speed Passenger Rail: Future Development Will Depend on Addressing Financial and Other Challenges and Establishing a Clear Federal Role*, GAO-09-317, March 2009, p. 10, http://www.gao.gov/new.items/d09317.pdf.

[7] In the FY2012 and FY2013 budgets, the Administration's request combined several rail programs into proposed new Network Development and System Preservation accounts.

Hence, it was not entirely clear how much was being requested for the formerly titled High Speed and Intercity Passenger Rail Program. In the FY2012 budget the total request for Network Development was $4 billion of which $3 billion appears to have been requested as part of an additional upfront investment of $50 billion for economic stimulus. In the FY2013 budget, $1 billion was requested for Network Development.

[8] "Maglev" stands for magnetic levitation, in which superconducting magnets levitate a train above a guide rail.

[9] International Union of Railways, "General Definitions of High speed," available at http://www.uic.asso.fr/gv/article.php3?id_article=14.

[10] Department of Transportation, Federal Railroad Administration, *High-Speed Ground Transportation for America,* September 1997, p. 2-2.

[11] Testimony of Joseph C. Szabo, Administrator, Federal Railroad Administration, U.S. Department of Transportation, before the U.S. Congress, House Committee on Transportation and Infrastructure, Subcommittee on Railroads, Pipelines and Hazardous Materials, *High-Speed Rail in the United States: Opportunities and Challenges,* 111th Cong., 1st sess., October 14, 2009, p. 9.

[12] Department of Transportation, Federal Railroad Administration, "U.S. Transportation Secretary Ray LaHood Announces $2.4 Billion for High Speed Rail Projects," Press Release, October 28, 2010, DOT 192-10, http://www.fra.dot.gov/Pages/press-releases/227.shtml.

[13] Department of Transportation, "U.S. Department of Transportation Redirects $1.195 Billion in High Speed Funds," Press Release, DOT 208-10, December 9, 2010, http://www.fra.dot.gov/Pages/press-releases/231.shtml; Department of Transportation, Federal Railroad Administration, High-Speed Intercity Passenger Rail (HSIPR) Program, 76 *Federal Register* 14443-14457, March 16, 2011, http://www.fra.dot.gov/rpd/downloads/March_2011_HSR_NOFA.pdf.

[14] Department of Transportation, Federal Railroad Administration, "High-Speed Intercity Passenger Rail Program: Federal Investment Highlights," February 3, 2012, http://www.fra.dot.gov/rpd/downloads/HSIPR_Federal_Investment_Highlights_20120203.pdf.

[15] Data provided to CRS by FRA, May 8, 2012.

[16] See Illinois Department of Transportation, "Illinois High Speed Rail: Chicago to St. Louis, Project Overview," http://www.idothsr.org/about/overview.aspx; and Illinois Department of Transportation, "Illinois High Speed Rail: Chicago to St. Louis, Fact Sheet Issue 2," May 7, 2011, http://www.idothsr.org/pdf/fact%20sheet%20%20february%202011.pdf.

[17] Department of Transportation, Federal Railroad Administration, "FRA High-Speed Intercity Passenger Rail (HSIPR) Program Funding Selection Summary," http://www.fra.dot.gov/rpd/downloads/Master_HSIPR_Selection_Sheet.pdf.

[18] The application for supplemental projects in the Chicago-St. Louis corridor states that the first round of improvements, those based on the 2004 Record of Decision (ROD), will reduce one-way trip time from 5 hours and 30 minutes to 5 hours. The 2004 ROD states that trip times would be reduced to between 4 hours and 4 hours and 30minutes. See Illinois Department of Transportation, *Il-Chicago-St. Louis Corridor Supplemental Projects: Service Development Plan,* April 4, 2011, p. 22, http://www.idothsr.org/pdf/IL_Chicago_St_Louis_Supplement_SDP_COMBINED_APPLICATION_r2.pdf.

[19] Ibid., p. 21.

[20] Illinois Department of Transportation, "Illinois High Speed Rail: Chicago to St. Louis, Fact Sheet Issue 4," December 28, 2011, http://www.idothsr.org/pdf/hsr%202011%20fact%20sheet_issue%204.pdf.

[21] For example, see U.S. Congress, House Committee on Transportation and Infrastructure, Subcommittee on Railroads, Pipelines, and Hazardous Materials, *California's High-Speed Rail Plan: Skyrocketing Costs & Project Concerns,* 112th Cong., 1st sess., December 15, 2011, http://transportation.house.gov/hearings/hearingdetail.aspx? NewsID=1475.

[22] California High Speed Rail Authority, *California High Speed Rail Program Draft 2012 Business Plan*, November 1, 2011, p. 3-5, http://www.cahighspeedrail.ca.gov/assets/0/152/302/c7912c84-0180-4ded-b27e-d8e6aab2a9a1.pdf.

[23] Ibid., p. ES-7.

[24] Ibid., p. 3-6.

[25] See, for example, Dan Walters, "It's Time to Kill California's Bullet Train Boondoggle," *Sacramento Bee*, January 8, 2012, the http://www.sacbee.com/2012/01/08/4170890/dan-walters-its-time-to-kill-californias.html.

[26] California High Speed Rail Authority, *California High Speed Rail Program Draft Revised 2012 Business Plan*, April 2, 2012, p. 3-10, http://www.cahighspeedrail.ca.gov/uploaded Files/Document_Repository/Business_Plans/Draft%20Revised%202012%20Business%20Plan(2).pdf.

[27] California High Speed Rail Authority, *California High Speed Rail Program Draft 2012 Business Plan*, Chapter 8.

[28] Legislative Analyst's Office, *High Speed Rail Authority: The Draft 2012 Business Plan and Funding Plan*, November 29, 2011, p. 7, http://www.lao.ca.gov/handouts/transportation/2011/HSRA_Business_Funding_plan_11_29_11.pdf; California High-Speed Rail Peer Review Group, January 3, 2012, pp. 3-4, http://www.cahsrprg.com/files/Commentson CHSRA2010FundingPlan.pdf.

[29] California High Speed Rail Authority, *California High Speed Rail Program Draft Revised 2012 Business Plan*, Chapter 7.

[30] Mac Taylor, *The 2012-13 Budget: Funding Requests for High-Speed Rail*, Legislative Analyst's Office, April 17, 2012, http://www.lao.ca.gov/analysis/2012/transportation/high-speed-rail-041712.pdf.

[31] U.S. Department of Transportation, Letter from John D. Pocari, Deputy Secretary of Transportation, to Roelef van Ark, Chief Executive Officer, California High Speed Rail Authority, January 3, 2012, http://www.cahighspeedrail.ca.gov/assets/0/152/302/9f61175c-f0a9-4bc6-87bd-4e541d558038.pdf.

[32] Richard White, "Fast Train to Nowhere," *New York Times*, April 24, 2011, http://www.nytimes.com/2011/04/24/opinion/24white.html; "California's High Speed Rail System is Going Nowhere Fast," Editorial, *The Washington Post*, November 13, 2011, http://www.washingtonpost.com/opinions/californias-high-speed-rail-system-is-going-nowherefast/2011/11/08/gIQAKni2IN_story.html. See also the California High-Speed Rail Peer Review Group, p. 6.

[33] California High Speed Rail Authority, *California High Speed Rail Program Draft Revised 2012 Business Plan*, p. ES-2.

[34] Either option could entail gaining access to privately owned freight railroad rights-of-way. See CRS Report R42512, *Passenger Train Access to Freight Railroad Track*, by John Frittelli.

[35] Passenger Rail Working Group of the National Surface Transportation Policy and Revenue Study Commission, *Vision for the Future: U.S. Intercity Passenger Rail Network Through 2050*, December 6, 2007, p. 31.

[36] Amtrak owns only 363 of the 457 miles of the Northeast Corridor; the remainder is owned by a number of states and commuter rail agencies. Douglas John Bowen, "Amtrak's NEC: healthy hybrid: the Western Hemisphere's busiest passenger rail route delivers a dazzling array of service unequalled by more glamorous global counterparts," *Railway Age*, August 2008.

[37] Government Accountability Office, *Intercity Passenger Rail: Amtrak's Management of Northeast Corridor Improvements Demonstrates Need for Applying Best Practices*, GAO-04-94, February 27, 2004, pp. 19-20.

[38] Passenger Rail Working Group, op. cit., p 31.

[39] Ariane Bernard, "French Train Breaks Rail Speed Record," *New York Times*, April 4, 2007.

[40] As train speeds increase, the benefit of even greater speeds diminishes. For example, increasing the average speed on a 240-mile route from 60 mph to 120 mph reduces the trip

time by two hours, from four hours to two; the next 60-mph increase, from 120 mph to 180 mph, only reduces the trip time by 40 minutes; the next 60 mph increase beyond that, from 180 mph to 240 mph, would reduce the trip time by only 20 minutes.

[41] Freight railroads in the United States commonly operate "double stack" trains hauling containers. These have a relatively high elevation, which would interfere with overhead electric catenary systems such as those used on the NEC and in many other countries. Most countries that use overhead catenaries to power trains do not allow double-stack freight traffic on such lines.

[42] Federal Railway Administration regulations require that rail lines rated for speeds above 150 mph have no at-grade crossings. 49 CFR 213.347(a).

[43] David Barboza and Sharon LaFraniere, "Crash Raises Questions on China's Push to Build High-Speed Passenger Rail Lines," *New York Times*, July 26, 2011; American Association of State Highway And Transportation Officials (AASHTO), "Basic Facts About High Speed/Intercity Passenger Rail," Updated September 7, 2011, http://www.highspeed-rail.org/Pages/BasicFacts.aspx.

[44] P.L. 110-432, Division A, §104.

[45] The Senate's surface transportation authorization legislation, MAP-21, would allow the DOT Secretary to extend the deadline to 2018 under certain circumstances; the House Transportation and Infrastructure Committee's proposed surface transportation authorization legislation, H.R. 7, would extend the deadline to 2020.

[46] Philip Brasor, "Japan's maglev on track for financial crash," *The Japan Times Online*, July 26, 2009, http://www.japantimes.co.jp/text/fd20090726pb.html.

[47] *The Japan Times Online*, "Tokyo-Osaka Maglev Gets State OK," May 28, 2011, http://www.japantimes.co.jp/text/ nn20110528a8.html.

[48] They are Japan's Tokyo-Osaka route and France's Paris-Lyon route, cited by Iñaki Barrón de Angoiti, director of high-speed rail at the International Union of Railways, in Victoria Burnett, "Spain's High-Speed Rail Offers Guideposts for U.S.," *The New York Times On the Web*, May 30, 2009.

[49] GAO, *High Speed Passenger Rail: Future Development Will Depend on Addressing Financial and Other Challenges and Establishing a Clear Federal Role*, March 2009, GAO-09-317, p. 24.

[50] Ibid., p. 25.

[51] DOT Inspector General, *Analysis of the Benefits of High-Speed Rail on the Northeast Corridor*, Report CC-2008- 091, June 26, 2008.

[52] For further discussion of this issue, see Transportation Research Board, *Multimodal Aspects of Statewide Transportation Planning*, NCHRP Synthesis 286, 2000, http://ntl.bts.gov/lib/

17000/17600/17654/PB2001102765.pdf; and GAO, *Surface Transportation: Many Factors Affect Investment Decisions*, GAO-04-744, June 2004.

[53] NCHRP Synthesis 286, p. 1.

[54] Bent Flyvbjerg, Mette Skamris Holm, and Soren Buhl, "Underestimating Costs in Public Works Projects: Error or Lie?," *Journal of the American Planning Association*, Summer 2002, vol. 68, no. 3. Rail projects in this study included high speed and conventional intercity rail projects as well as rail transit projects.

[55] Defined as arriving within 10 minutes of the scheduled arrival time.

[56] Defined as arriving within 20 minutes of the scheduled arrival time.

[57] Amtrak, Monthly Performance Report for September 2011, p. E-7, http://www.amtrak.com/servlet/ContentServer?c=Page&pagename=am%2FLayout&cid=1241245669222.

[58] Andrew Nash, "Best Practices in Shared-Use High-Speed Rail Systems," Mineta Transportation Institute, June 2003.

[59] See CRS Report R42512, *Passenger Train Access to Freight Railroad Track*, by John Frittelli.

[60] One freight operator, Florida East Coast Railway, is reportedly interested in operating its own passenger service over track it owns or would build, but it is unclear whether this would be

a high speed service or would be viable without an operating subsidy. See http://jacksonville.com/news/metro/2012-06-04/story/company-offer-passenger-rail-miami-orlando-possible-expansion.

[61] For further information and analysis on economic viability, see DOT IG, *FRA Needs to Expand Its Guidance on High Speed Rail Project Viability Assessments,* Report no. CR-2012-083, March 28, 2012.

[62] Transportation Research Board, *In Pursuit of Speed: New Options for Intercity Passenger Transport* (Washington, DC: National Research Council, 1991), p. 113.; Ginés de Rus and Gustavo Nombela, "Is Investment in High Speed Rail Socially Profitable?," *Journal of Transport Economics and Policy,* vol. 41, no. 1 (January 2007), p. 15; Ginés de Rus and Chris Nash, "In What Circumstances is Investment in HSR Worthwhile?," chapter 3 of *Economic Analysis of High Speed Rail In Europe,* Ginés de Rus (ed.), Bilbao, 2009, p. 70.

[63] Amtrak, *Monthly Performance Report for September 2011,* November 2, 2011, p. A-3.5, http://www.amtrak.com/servlet/ContentServer?c=Page&pagename=am%2FLayout&cid=1241245 669222. Amtrak's slower service in the Northeast Corridor, the Northeast Regional, carried 7.5 million passengers; fares for the Northeast Regional Service are less than half those charged for Acela service. Only five other Amtrak routes nationwide carried more than 1 million passengers in FY2011.

[64] Based on FY2010, 3rd quarter data. Amtrak Government Affairs Department, "Amtrak's Northeast Corridor: FY2010," May 2011.

[65] Ibid., pp. 10-14.

[66] Amtrak, *National Fact Sheet: FY2010,* http://www.amtrak.com/servlet/ContentServer?c=Page &pagename=am%2FLayout&cid=1246041980246.

[67] According to U.S. Census 2005 data, 55.1% of occupied housing units in New York City do not keep a vehicle available at home for personal use. U.S. Census, *County and City Data Book: 2007,* 14th edition (latest edition available). The only other cities with at least a third of households not having a vehicle are also in the Northeast Corridor: Washington, DC, Boston, and Philadelphia.

[68] For an argument on this point, see California High Speed Rail Authority, "Moving California Forward: California's High-Speed Train System," http://www.cahighspeedrail.ca.gov/news/MOBILITY_lr.pdf.

[69] U.S. Department of Transportation, Federal Railroad Administration, *High-Speed Ground Transportation forAmerica,* Washington, DC, September 1997, p. 7-8, http://www.fra.dot.gov/Downloads/RRDev/cfs0997all2.pdf.

[70] U.S. Department of Transportation, Office of the Secretary of Transportation, Office of the Inspector General, *Analysis of the Benefits of High Speed Rail on the Northeast Corridor,* Washington, DC, June 26, 2008, http://www.oig.dot.gov/sites/dot/files/pdfdocs/HSR_Final_7-1-08.pdf.

[71] U.S. Department of Transportation, Federal Railroad Administration and Florida High Speed Rail Authority, *Final Environmental Impact Statement: Florida High Speed Rail, Tampa to Orlando,* May 2005, p. 1-7, 4-119, http://www.fra.dot.gov/downloads/RRDev/florida_tampa-orlando_feis.pdf.

[72] IG, 2008, p. 3.

[73] Randal O' Toole, *High-Speed Rail: the Wrong Road for America,* Cato Institute, Policy Analysis, No. 625, October 31, 2008, p. 8, http://www.cato.org/pubs/pas/pa-625.pdf.

[74] See, for example, the cost estimates for NextGen in Government Accountability Office, Next Generation Air Transportation System: Status of Systems Acquisition and the Transition to the Next Generation Air Transportation System, GAO-08-1078, Washington, DC, September 2008, p.7, http://www.gao.gov/new.items/d081078.pdf.

[75] See, for example, Center for Clean Air Policy and Center for Neighborhood Technology, *High Speed Rail and Greenhouse Gas Emissions in the U.S.,* January 2006, http://www.cnt.org/repository/HighSpeedRailEmissions.pdf, and California High Speed Rail Authority,

"California High-Speed Train System Environmental Protection," http://www.cahighspeedrail.ca.gov/news/Factsheetenviro.pdf.

[76] HM Treasury and Department for Transport, *The Eddington Transport Study: Main Report, Volume 3*, London, 2006, p. 213, http://www.dft.gov.uk/about/strategy/transportstrategy/eddingtonstudy/.

[77] Jan-Eric Nilsson and Roger Pyddoke, *High-Speed Railways—A Climate Policy Sidetrack*. VTI (Swedish National Road and Transport Research) #655, 2009, p. 13, http://www.vti.se/en/publications/high-speed-railways--a-climatepolicy-sidetrack/.

[78] Eddington Transport Study, 2006, p. 211.

[79] CRS Report R40104, *Economic Stimulus: Issues and Policies*, by Jane G. Gravelle, Thomas L. Hungerford, and Marc Labonte.

[80] California High Speed Rail Authority, "Project Vision and Scope," http://www.cahighspeedrail.ca.gov/project_vision.aspx.

[81] Ibid.

[82] Jerry Nickelsburg and Saurabh Ahluwalia, "California High-Speed Rail and Economic Development: Lessons from Japan," *UCLA Anderson Forecast*, June 2012, p. 107, http://www.anderson.ucla.edu/documents/areas/ctr/forecast/UCLAForecast_June2012_HSR.pdf.

[83] U.S. Government Accountability Office, *High Speed Passenger Rail*, GAO-09-317, March 2009, Washington, DC, p. 29, http://www.gao.gov/new.items/d09317.pdf.

[84] Eddington Transport Study, 2006, p. 208.

[85] See, for example, U.S. Department of Transportation, Bureau of Transportation Statistics, *Transportation Statistics Annual Report 1997*, Washington, DC, 1997, pp. 22-23, http://www.bts.gov/publications/transportation_statistics_annual_report/1997/pdf/report.pdf.

[86] See, for example, U.S. Department of Transportation, Research and Special Programs Administration, Effects of Catastrophic Events on Transportation System Management and Operations: Cross Cutting Study, January 2003, http://www.itsdocs.fhwa.dot.gov//JPODOCS/REPTS_TE//13780_files/13780.pdf.

[87] TranSystems, *Chicago to St. Louis 220 mph High Speed Rail Alternative Corridor Study*, October 8, 2008, http://www.midwesthsr.org/sites/default/files/pdf/MHSRA_Chicago_StLouis_HSR_Corridor_Study.pdf.

[88] U.S. Congress, House Committee on Transportation and Infrastructure, *The Surface Transportation Authorization Act of 2009: A Blueprint for Investment and Reform*, Executive Summary, 111th Cong., 1st sess., June 18, 2009, p. 4, available at http://transportation.house.gov/Media/file/Highways/HPP/Surface%20Transportation%20Blueprint%20Executive%20Summary.pdf.

[89] As noted earlier, congressional support for HSR changed significantly as a result of the 2010 midterm election; in the two years prior to that election, Congress had appropriated $10.5 billion for passenger rail, including HSR; in the year after that election, Congress provided no additional funding, and cut $400 million of the funding already appropriated.

[90] This would be a grade separated, dedicated double-tracked passenger-only line of approximately 200 miles that would generally follow the I-15 corridor. The developer, DesertXpress Enterprises, describes the project as a public/private partnership, since it hopes to use public right-of-way (http://www.desertxpress.com/economics.php). DesertXpress has applied for a $4.9 billion loan from the Railroad Rehabilitation and Improvement Financing Program to help finance the $6 billion project. See "DesertXpress hopes for federal loan, aims for 2012 start on work," *Las Vegas Sun*, October 10, 2011.

[91] Prospects for High Speed Rail in the U.S., presentation prepared by Mercer Management Consulting before the House Committee on Transportation and Infrastructure, March 20, 2007.

[92] U.S. Department of Transportation, *Budget Highlights: Fiscal Year 2013*, Washington, DC, 2012, p.32, http://www.dot.gov/budget/2013/dot_budget_highlights_fy_2013.pdf.

[93] While the federal share for new rail transit projects receiving funding through the Federal Transit Administration's New Starts program can, by statute, be up to 80%; in practice the

average federal share is lower; FTA has encouraged applicants to provide a local match of more than 20%, and since FY2002 the Senate Committee on Appropriations has directed FTA not to provide more than a 60% federal match.

[94] FRA has published a Preliminary National Rail Plan and a National Rail Plan Progress Report. The preliminary plan is described as setting forth FRA's proposed approach to developing the long-range National Rail Plan, including providing background information and identifying issues that FRA believes should be considered in developing National Rail Plan. Federal Railroad Administration, *Preliminary National Rail Plan: The Groundwork for Developing Policies to Improve the United States Transportation System*, October 15, 2009, http://www.fra.dot.gov/Downloads/RailPlanPrelim10-15.pdf. The progress report is a product of 15 months of study and discussions with partners in the rail industry. Federal Railroad Administration, National Rail Plan: Moving Forward, A Progress Report, September 2010, http://www.fra.dot.gov/downloads/NRP_Sept2010_WEB.pdf.

[95] In Japan, high speed rail is referred to as *Shinkansen* (literally, "New Trunk Line"). The trains are often called "bullet trains" because of their shape and speed, though the term *Shinkansen* is often used to refer to the trains as well as the railway.

[96] International Union of Railways, *High-Speed Rail Lines in the World, Updated 1st November, 2011*, http://www.uic.org/spip.php?article573.

[97] Réseau Ferré de France, *[Rail] Network Inventory*, http://www.rff.fr/pages/reseau/inventaire_reseau.asp?lg=en.

[98] U.S. Congress, House Committee on Transportation and Infrastructure, Subcommittee on Railroads, Pipelines, and Hazardous Materials, Testimony of Jean Marie Metzler, French National Railroads, 110th Cong., 1st sess., April 19, 2007, http://republicans.transportation.house.gov/Media/File/Testimony/Rail/4-19-07-Metzler. pdf.

[99] Heike Link, "German Railway Reform: Chances and Risks," *Japan Railway & Transport Review*, June 1994, p. 22.

[100] Available at http://www.fomento.es/MFOMWeb/paginas/buscar.aspx.

[101] Giles Tremlett, "Spain's high-speed trains win over fed-up flyers," *The Guardian*, January 13, 2009.

[102] Though its population is approximately four times larger than that of the United States, China's railway network is less than half the size of the U.S. rail network (the same is true of its highway network). *EU Energy and Transport inFigures 2009*, p. 105, http://ec.europa.eu/energy/publications/statistics/doc/2009_energy_transport_figures.pdf.

[103] Keith Bradsher, "High Speed Rail Poised to Alter China," *New York Times*, June 22, 2011.

[104] *Wall Street Journal*, "Rail Line Collapses in China," March 13, 2012, http://online.wsj.com/article/SB10001424052702304537904577277200065540834.html.

[105] Shima, Takashi, "Taiwan High Speed Rail," *Japan Railway and Transport Review* 48, August 2007, p. 40,http://www.jrtr.net/jrtr48/pdf/f40_Shi.pdf.

[106] http://www.railway-technology.com/projects/taiwan/.

[107] Shima, Takashi, "Taiwan High Speed Rail," *Japan Railway and Transport Review* 48, August 2007, p. 45,http://www.jrtr.net/jrtr48/pdf/f40_Shi.pdf.

[108] Ministry of Transportation and Communications, Monthly Statistics of Transportation and Communication, Table 2-8: Passenger Traffic of High-Speed Rail, http://210.69.99.7/mocwebGIP/wSite/ct?xItem=4882&ctNode=213&mp=2.

[109] "Government Takes Over to Keep High Speed Rail on Track," September 28, 2009, http://www.cens.com/cens/html/en/news/news_inner_29333.html.

[110] "High Speed Rail is a Money Making Venture," *International Railway Journal*, September 23, 2011; http://www.railjournal.com/this-month/high-speed-rail-is-a-money-making-venture-1328.html.

[111] Ahn B.O., Korail director of International Affairs, quoted in "High Speed Rail Boosts South Korea's Business," *ABC News*, November 15, 2011, http://abclocal.go.com/kgo/story?section=news/assignment_7&id=8433340.

[112] Jeong Gwan Lee, spokesperson for the Korean Consul General in San Francisco, cited in "High Speed Rail Boosts South Korea's Business," *ABC News*, November 15, 2011, http://abclocal.go.com/kgo/story?section=news/assignment_7&id=8433340.

[113] Bechtel, Korea High Speed Rail, http://www.bechtel.com/assets/files/PDF/Rail/Rail_KoreaHSR.pdf.

In: Railroads in the United States   ISBN: 978-1-62257-727-9
Editors: Ch. E. Russel and C. M. Wood © 2013 Nova Science Publishers, Inc.

Chapter 2

PASSENGER TRAIN ACCESS TO FREIGHT RAILROAD TRACK[*]

John Frittelli

SUMMARY

Pressure is building for greater passenger use of freight railroad rights of way. Freight railroad rights of way are owned by private, for-profit corporations, and the routes potentially most useful for passenger service are typically the busiest with freight traffic. In many cases, states or commuter rail authorities have reached agreement with freight railroads to share either their track or right of way. However, unlike Amtrak, which has eminent domain power over freight facilities and can appeal to a federal agency to determine the terms of its access to freight track, other would-be passenger rail operators do not have any statutory leverage when negotiating with freight railroads. This likely increases the price public authorities pay for access and leaves them with no apparent recourse when freight railroads reject their offers.

During House committee mark-up of the Passenger Rail Investment and Improvement Act of 2008 (P.L. 110-432), a provision to require binding arbitration when commuter rail authorities and freight railroads fail to reach

---

[*] This is an edited, reformatted and augmented version of the Congressional Research Service Publication, CRS Report for Congress R42512, dated May 2, 2012.

agreement over access proved controversial. The committee chose instead to require non-binding arbitration. Some Members of Congress have urged greater reliance on private companies to provide intercity rail services similar to those offered by Amtrak, but such private services may be difficult to develop so long as potential operators lack Amtrak's statutory right to compel freight railroads to carry passenger trains. Freight railroads can be expected to object to such initiatives as unfair "takings" of their private property. In the 112th Congress, the version of surface transportation legislation passed by the Senate (S. 1813) calls for a federal study to evaluate passenger service in shared-use rail corridors and to survey processes for resolving disputes over passenger access.

Passenger access to freight railroad track raises old but recurring questions about the fundamental nature of railroad rights of way. Railroads are not like other businesses that are free to decide how and where they allocate resources solely on the principle of maximizing shareholder returns. While railroad rights of way are private property, more than a century of case law has upheld a public duty on them. The public nature of railroads is evident from the fact that they were designated as "common carriers," granted eminent domain power, and regulated by government. However, the private interest of railroads is protected by the limitation that the government's right to regulate does not mean the right to confiscate. Railroad rights of way, unlike highways, were not considered part of the "public domain." When competition from other modes eroded passenger rail travel, it was confirmed that the public duty attached to railroads could obligate them to operate some trains at a loss, provided the railroad's overall operations were profitable.

The issue for Congress is whether freight railroads and prospective passenger rail authorities should negotiate over the terms of use of railroad property just as any private parties would or if a governmental third party, such as the federal Surface Transportation Board (STB), should have some role in determining the terms. Given that a public service obligation is still attached to railroads, albeit largely lifted with respect to passenger service, do freight railroads have the right to set the price for passenger access unilaterally, or should the public's convenience and necessity be given some consideration? Granting track access rights to potential private operators of passenger service could be a particularly thorny issue. Given the increasing demands on urban rail corridors, Congress might examine alternative methods for managing them. A public "rail port authority" might have some advantages over private railroads in optimizing an urban rail network.

INTRODUCTION

Pressure is building for passenger train use of freight railroad rights of way. Congress has provided substantial federal funding for new high-speed and intercity passenger rail services, and many state and local governments are interested in expanding both intercity and commuter routes. In most cases, such proposed services would use trackage controlled by privately owned freight railroads or build new tracks within a freight railroad's right of way.

Amtrak, the federally owned rail passenger operator, has eminent domain power over freight railroad facilities and can appeal to a federal adjudicator, the Surface Transportation Board (STB),[1] to determine the terms of its access to freight railroad track.[2] This is not the case for other current or potential passenger rail operators. Such operators, whether intercity or commuter, can use rail freight corridors only if they reach agreements with the freight railroads that own or lease the rights of way. Those agreements typically involve public funding to add track capacity and upgrade infrastructure for passenger trains, thereby facilitating freight operations as well. Changes in passenger operations, such as an increase in the number of trains or in train speeds, are likely to require additional negotiations. As passenger operators other than Amtrak have no statutory leverage when negotiating with freight railroads,[3] they have little control over the price of access and may have no recourse if freight railroads reject their proposals.

The tension between commuter and freight use of track was highlighted during mark-up of the Passenger Rail Investment and Improvement Act of 2008 (P.L. 110-432). During House committee mark-up, a provision (§401) to require binding arbitration when commuter rail authorities and freight railroads fail to reach agreement over access proved controversial. The committee chose instead to require non-binding arbitration, leaving the possibility that the public authority might be unable to implement a proposed commuter-rail project. In the 112th Congress, the Senate-passed version of surface transportation reauthorization legislation (S. 1813) calls for the U.S. Department of Transportation to evaluate the best means to enhance intercity passenger service in shared-use rail corridors and to survey processes for resolving disputes over passenger access.

If interest in passenger rail services continues to grow, Congress is likely to hear proposals to grant passenger interests greater bargaining power with freight railroads. Some commuter rail authorities and advocates of intercity passenger trains have suggested granting states or commuter authorities the same access rights Amtrak "enjoys."[4] Some Members of Congress have urged greater reliance on private companies to provide intercity rail services similar to those offered by Amtrak, but such private services may be difficult to develop so long as potential operators lack Amtrak's statutory right to compel freight railroads to allow passenger trains to use their tracks. Freight railroads can be expected to object to such initiatives as unfair "takings" of their private property.

RECENT ACCESS NEGOTIATIONS

Recent examples illustrate the range of disputes that can arise in negotiations between freight and would-be passenger rail operators. Union Pacific Railroad has emphatically stated to the California High Speed Rail Authority that it has no room for proposed passenger trains on, over, or alongside its freight rights of way.[5] Even building high-speed tracks alongside its right of way, Union Pacific states, would create a barrier to any future rail-served development on that side. In upstate New York, a project for higher speed intercity service between Albany and Buffalo has been delayed by disagreement with the host freight railroad over the amount of space needed between freight and passenger tracks for safe operation, as well as disagreement over the speed the passenger trains would be allowed to operate.[6] The freight railroad's requirements would severely curtail passenger rail operations. The city of Denver at one time was contemplating building a light rail passenger line on city streets because a freight railroad objected, on safety grounds, to mixing lighter passenger rail cars with heavy freight rail cars over the same rail corridor.[7] More recently, it was announced that the city may have to substitute bus rapid transit for commuter rail service over part of a route due, in part, to higher unanticipated costs associated with acquiring a freight line.[8] City of Boston officials have been frustrated over decade-long negotiations with a freight railroad to purchase tracks to improve commuter rail service into the city.[9] The city and railroad disagreed over the appropriate methodology for valuing the right of way land. The city of Orlando just recently reached agreement with a freight railroad over the purchase price for track to be used for new commuter rail service.[10] As part of the agreement, the freight railroad is to invest the proceeds from the sale in freight facilities within Florida.

RAILROADS: PUBLIC PURPOSES BUT PRIVATE PROPERTY

Mandating passenger-train access to freight rights of way raises old but recurring arguments about the fundamental nature of privately owned railroads. A long line of court decisions holds that while railroads are not charities, neither are they completely like other businesses that are free to operate solely for profit maximization.[11] Railroads are not free to leave the business at will or use their property for some other purpose. In other words, while railroad rights of way are private property, there is substantial case law that has infused them with a public interest or a public duty component. The remainder of this chapter provides historical context to the conflict between private and public interests in railroading. The arguments made over which of these competing interests should be preferred or how far one should be made subservient to the other are relevant, and inform the present policy debate.

The first railroads in the United States were built for the purpose of moving cargo. In the 1850s, the typical railroad received only a quarter to a third of its total revenue from passenger travel. Some railroads, typically shorter lines, ran "mixed" trains carrying both passengers and freight.[12]

Commuter service was first recognized by railroads as a no-cost means of additional revenue for those intercity passenger trains whose schedules happened to coincide with rush hour traffic. Railroads offered "commuted" (reduced) fares to these passengers, recognizing that the normal fare was too high for traveling twice a day, six days per week. In the largest cities, this service became popular and railroads began operating dedicated commuter trains. Commuter trains typically operated at a loss because trips were too short and business was too concentrated at rush hours; equipment and labor were idle the rest of the day. They also lacked one source of revenue that was significant for intercity passenger trains, mail delivery. The economic return for commuter trains came from suburban residential development on land controlled directly or indirectly by the railroads. An indication of how irrelevant commuter fares were to the railroads' investment in this service was a 1911 survey which found that some railroads had not raised fares for 15 to 30 years, and in a few instances for as long as 40 years.[13]

Typically, railroads were chartered by the states, a fact relevant to a later debate about federal versus state control. A requirement that a railroad provide passenger service was often stated in its charter, or could be stated in the state's constitution, or in state statute. In order not to compete with the Erie

Canal, the charter for the Utica and Schenectady Railroad Co. forbade it from
carrying anything but passengers. Other railroads chartered in upstate New
York could only carry cargo in the winter when the canal was closed.[14]

Unlike other businesses, railroads were under a legal obligation to serve
the public and could not discontinue operations without government approval.
They were regarded as "common carriers," a concept originating in English
law in the middle ages (with precursors as far back as the Roman commercial
code) that invoked duties of a public nature.[15]

In their charters, the government often gave railroads eminent domain
power. This authority signifies the quasi-public nature of railroads, because
eminent domain powers were only granted to achieve a public purpose. An
1837 New York court ruling upholding a railroad's power of eminent domain
described the dual nature of railroads. A private property owner had
challenged a chartered upstate New York railroad's authority to acquire his
land since the railroad would be operated for private profit. The court reasoned
that the fact that the railroad was privately owned and was entitled to charge
for its services did not alter the public nature of the enterprise. The court
stated,[16] "Because the legislature permitted the company to remunerate itself
for the expense of constructing the road, from those who should travel upon it,
its private character is not established; it does not destroy the public nature of
the road, or convert it from a public to a private use."

This court also supported the public nature of railroad rights of way by
noting that the railroad could be prosecuted if it refused to transport a person
or his property without a reasonable excuse and that the legislature had the
power to regulate the prices charged by the railroad.

The Rise of Regulation

During their golden age prior to World War I, when railroads had a near-
monopoly on intercity transportation, states became concerned with monopoly
abuses by the railroads. Railroads, not surprisingly, challenged the authority of
state governments. These cases, which eventually went to the Supreme Court,
addressed the fundamental issue of whether privately owned railroad rights of
way were under railroads' exclusive control or whether their character made
them quasi-public institutions in which the public has an interest.[17] These cases
are important to present-day concerns about public access to freight railroad
rights of way because eventually they established three important principles:

GLOSSARY

Common carrier—a railroad that holds itself out to the general public to transport property or passengers for compensation and must do so upon reasonable request for service.

Right of way—the strip of land on which railroad track is built. A railroad could own the strip of land as real property or it could own a mere easement which is the right/privilege to run trains over the strip of land.

Eminent domain—a right of government to take private property with just compensation for public use by virtue of its sovereignty over all lands within its jurisdiction.

Condemn—to declare property convertible to public use under the right of eminent domain.

Abandonment—a railroad terminates all service over a line. The right of way land may be sold and its clear path lost as the land is used for other purposes. Railroad regulatory jurisdiction over the line ceases as well.

Discontinuance—a railroad terminates some service over a line, like passenger service, but maintains other service over the line (such as freight).

Class I railroads—the seven large U.S. freight railroads whose networks extend over vast regions and account for about 70% of U.S. railroad mileage. Class II and III railroads are regional and shortline railroads, respectively.

Police power—the inherent power of state governments, often delegated in part to local governments, to impose upon private rights those restrictions that are reasonably related to promotion of the health, safety, morals, and general welfare of the public.

Sources: John H. Armstrong, *The Railroad-What It Is, What It Does*, 4th ed., 1998; *Barron's Law Dictionary*, 5th ed., 2003.

- the public does have a right to some amount of control over rights of way;
- this public control is vested predominantly in the federal government, not the states, because railroads are intrinsically an *inter*state means of commerce;
- this control does not give the public the right to confiscate.

Public Interest

In *Munn v. Illinois* (1876), the Supreme Court upheld a state's authority to regulate those particular categories of business whose property was "clothed with a public interest." The Court stated,[18] "When the owner of property devotes it to a use in which the public has an interest, he in effect grants to the public an interest in such use, and must to the extent of that interest, submit to be controlled by the public, for the common good, as long as he maintains the use."

The Court also reasoned that common carriers are held to "exercise a sort of public office, and have public duties to perform."

Two judges dissenting in this case foreshadowed an argument that held sway in the next century when passenger trains became unprofitable and railroads petitioned to discontinue them. The dissenting judges argued that almost all private businesses could be considered as having an element of public interest and that for the legislature to regulate their prices was a taking of private property without due process. If a property owner "is compelled to take as compensation for its use less than the expenses to which he is subjected by its ownership, he is, for all practical purposes, deprived of the property, as effectually as if the legislature had ordered his forcible dispossession."[19]

Federal versus State Control

A decade later, the Supreme Court essentially overturned *Munn v. Illinois*, necessitating establishment of a federal role in regulating railroad rates and service. In *Wabash, St. Louis and Pacific Railway Company v. Illinois* (1886),[20] a railroad challenged the authority of the Illinois state railroad commission to regulate the Illinois portion of a rate for shipments between points within Illinois and New York. The Court reasoned that this regulation by the state affected interstate commerce, which only the federal government had authority to regulate. The Court focused on the onerous conditions that would be imposed on railroads if each state provided rules applicable to its own passengers and freight regardless of the interests of others.

In response to the *Wabash* ruling, Congress created the Interstate Commerce Commission (ICC) in 1887, modeling it after state railroad commissions.[21] (Numerous bills related to railroad regulation had been introduced in Congress since 1868.) In the ICC Act, Congress impressed the common carrier concept upon both freight and passenger railroad service: "the provisions of this act shall apply to any common carrier or carriers engaged in the transportation of passengers or property wholly by railroad" and further stated that "Every common carrier subject to the provisions of this act shall, according to their respective powers, afford all reasonable, proper, and equal facilities ... for the receiving, forwarding and delivering of passengers and property."

Limits to Government Power

In 1890, the Supreme Court limited governments' power to regulate railroad rates, holding that rates cannot be made so unreasonably low as to deprive the railroad company of any chance of profit; the right to regulate, the court held, was not the right to confiscate.[22] State legislators or regulators had tended to set low rates on local traffic, which had the effect of shifting the cost of providing railroad service to interstate shippers, undermining the national interest in a viable national railroad network.[23] Subsequent court cases strengthened the ICC while narrowing the scope of state authority. A 1914 Supreme Court ruling upheld the ICC's authority over *intra*state rates that were found to be injurious to *inter*state commerce.[24] There was also a practical limit to state governments' imposition of unremunerative rates, as some railroad companies closed down their operations to avoid being forced to "pour their money into a hole in the ground."[25]

In 1906, under the Hepburn Act,[26] Congress granted the ICC additional powers, and placed certain railroad activities that may have been contracted out, such as express and sleeping car services, under the common carrier umbrella. The law further stated, "it shall be the duty of every carrier subject to the provisions of the Act to provide and furnish such transportation upon reasonable request."

Local Passenger Station Stoppage Laws

One of the requirements for profitable railroad operation is traffic density. Railroads can achieve better economies by limiting stops to locations that offer a substantial customer base. Consequently, access to railroad rights of way by smaller communities, smaller shippers, and/or those seeking travel for relatively short distances has been a long-standing issue. These customers have relied on legal principles of "fairness" to gain access to the railroad network.

At the turn of the last century, the Supreme Court, in a series of cases, held that railroads were obligated to provide local service as long as this requirement was enforced in such a way that it did not impede interstate commerce.[27] For instance, the Supreme Court struck down an Illinois law that required all passenger trains to stop at every county seat.[28] The Court pronounced this an unconstitutional hindrance of commerce because the trains were also providing express mail delivery. A 1907 Missouri law requiring that all passenger trains stop at junction points with other railroads was struck down on similar grounds.[29]

On the other hand, the Supreme Court upheld a Minnesota stoppage law because it distinguished between local passenger trains and interstate through trains.[30] *Gladstone v. Minnesota* involved passenger train service between St. Paul and Duluth. The Minnesota law required *intra*state passenger trains to stop at every county seat on their course but expressly exempted the *inter*state through trains from this requirement. In upholding this law the Court referred to a state's "police power" as the basis for a state's authority to regulate intrastate trains.

One notable ruling on the obligations of railroads to provide local passenger service to less densely populated communities came in 1899, when a sharply divided Supreme Court upheld an Ohio law requiring railroads to stop at least three passenger trains daily (travelling in each direction) at villages with more than 3,000 inhabitants.[31] The Court found that this was not an unreasonable burden on interstate trains because the railroads were free to schedule other trains on an express basis. The majority held that a state's police power, in addition to providing for the public health, public morals, and public safety of its citizens, also included providing for "public convenience":[32]

> [The state of Ohio] was not compelled to look only to the convenience of those who desired to pass through the State without stopping. Any other view of the relations between the State and the corporation created by it [the railroad] would mean that the Directors of the corporation could manage its affairs solely with reference to the interests of stockholders and without taking into consideration the interests of the general public. It would mean not only that such directors were the exclusive judges of the

manner in which the corporation should discharge the duties imposed upon it in the interest of the public, but that the corporation could so regulate the running of its interstate trains as to build up cities and towns at the ends of its line or at favored points, and by that means destroy or retard the growth and prosperity of those at intervening points.

Police power remains an important issue in the debate about the extent of local control over railroad operations. Over the past century, Congress has reduced but not eliminated the ability of state or local governments to control railroads operating in their jurisdictions, and the distinction between a reasonable exercise of local police power and an unreasonable interference with commerce continues to be contentious.[33]

Balancing the Needs of Travelers and Shippers

One of the policy questions associated with granting states or localities a right to access railroad rights of way is whether they would give due consideration to both freight and passenger interests. Since freight does not vote, one might speculate that passenger interests would inevitably be favored. On the other hand, cities (especially port cities) recognize that convenient rail connections are important for attracting commerce.

In the current era, freight railroads have been moving many of their urban intermodal yards to the suburbs or exurbs, where they can have sufficient space for container storage and avoid the expense of constructing overhead clearances through the urban core for taller double-stack container trains.[34] This shift can free up track for passenger use. In Boston, a city with a strong passenger rail tradition, CSX railroad has sold most of its rights of way to the Massachusetts Bay Transportation Authority for commuter-train operations, but container cargo must now be trucked over 40 miles between the port and the CSX terminal in Worcester, MA.[35] In Chicago, where both freight and passenger rail have strong traditions, a major project is underway to build overpasses or underpasses to better accommodate freight trains through the city, reducing conflicts at numerous grade-crossings.[36] One of the motivations for this project is to prevent additional freight yards (and rail jobs) from moving to the exurbs.[37] These examples indicate that different states and cities might balance passenger and shipper interests differently.

The Supreme Court Justices in the 1899 Ohio stoppage law case disagreed whether local governments could adequately balance the needs of both passengers and shippers. Justices in the majority argued that local governments could manage the rights of way in their jurisdiction more wisely than a distant federal authority. Justices in the minority argued that local governments would discount the needs of national commerce. The majority opinion cited as precedent an 1882 case that involved balancing the needs of passengers and shippers in Chicago.[38] A city ordinance had prescribed that drawbridges over the Chicago River not be opened during rush hours and not be opened for more than 10 minutes at a time during the rest of the day (Sundays excepted). A barge carrier sued. The Supreme Court upheld the Chicago ordinance as "just and reasonable." But in a ruling that would be widely cited, it also made clear that the city's control over the bridges was not absolute:

> Illinois is more immediately affected by the bridges over the Chicago River and its branches than any other State, and is more directly concerned for the prosperity of the city of Chicago, for the convenience and comfort of its inhabitants, and the growth of its commerce. And nowhere could the power to control the bridges in that city, their construction, form, and strength, and the size of their draws, and the manner and times of using them, be better vested than with the State, or the authorities of the city upon whom it has devolved that duty. When its power is exercised, so as to unnecessarily obstruct the navigation of the river or its branches, Congress may interfere and remove the obstruction. If the power of the State and that of the Federal government come in conflict, the latter must control and the former yield.

The four Justices dissenting in the Ohio stoppage law case argued that the Ohio law discriminated against national interests in favor of local interests. The dissenting Justices quoted at length from the *Wabash v. Illinois* decision, arguing that the regulation of commerce must of necessity be of a national, not local, character. The dissenting judges argued,

> It is fallacious ... to contend that the Ohio legislation in question was enacted to promote the public interest. That can only mean the public interest of the State of Ohio, and the reason why such legislation is pernicious and unsafe is because it is based upon a discrimination in favor of local interests, and is hostile to the larger public interest and convenience involved in interstate commerce. Practically there may be no real or considerable conflict between the public interest that is local and that which is general. But, as the state legislatures are controlled by those who represent local demands, their action frequently results in measures detrimental to the interests of the greater public, and hence it is that the people of the United States have, by their constitution and the

acts of Congress, removed the control and regulation of interstate commerce from the state legislatures.

In another case, the Supreme Court recognized the competitive environment among railroads on intercity routes, and judged as unfair a local stoppage law that would hinder one railroad from competing with its rivals.[39] Magnolia, MS, had petitioned to have intercity passenger trains traveling between New Orleans and Chicago stop in the town. The Court struck down this stoppage law, stating,[40]

> Competition between great trunk lines is fierce and at times bitter. Each line must do its best even to obtain its fair share of the transportation between States, both of passengers and freight. A wholly unnecessary, even though a small, obstacle ought not, in fairness, to be placed in the way of an interstate road, which may thus be unable to meet the competition of its rivals.

The ruling in the Mississippi case remains relevant today because most large cities have at least two trunk line (Class I) railroads in direct competition. Thus, if a state or municipality were to require one of the railroads to accommodate commuter or intercity passenger trains in its right of way, that requirement could affect the competitive situation between the two rivals.

Local station stoppage laws at the turn of the last century point to the conflict between interstate and local users of a railroad network that was rapidly becoming national in scope. Perhaps for this reason, an entirely separate railroad network was constructed to serve local travelers. Between 1890 and World War I, more than 18,000 miles of interurban electric railroads were built, mostly with a different gage than steam track to preclude access by freight trains. Interurban trains typically consisted of just one or two passenger cars making frequent stops. By 1933, more than half of this network had already been abandoned due to auto and bus travel.

The *raison d'être* of the interurban electric network raises a fundamental question: can today's railroad network, North American in scope, adequately serve both local and long-distance users? Even shortline freight railroads, typically hauling small amounts of cargo for short distances, complain today about difficulty accessing the transcontinental network.[41] The Class I (transcontinental) freight railroads can better exploit their comparative advantage over other modes by moving entire train loads of the same cargo from one origin to one destination, rather than stopping to pick up or drop off single-carload shipments along the way.[42] Use of their track for local purposes might therefore interfere with the Class I railroads' business strategies.

Condemning Railroad Property for Other Public Uses

Although railroads were delegated eminent domain power because they would be providing a public good, a series of cases also established that railroad property can be condemned for the purpose of providing a second public good. These cases describe the circumstances under which passenger operators might possibly condemn portions of railroad rights of way. In many situations, freight railroads are not using the entire widths of their rights of way, having taken advantage of advances in signal technology and other efficiencies to run single-track rather than double-track operations. For example, outside the Northeast Corridor, 70% of the freight-owned mileage over which Amtrak operates is single tracked. In addition, 6 of Amtrak's 12 shorter-distance corridor routes operate on rights of way that are at least 70% single tracked.[43] The following cases suggest that demands to take unused land within railroad rights of way for passenger service might be subject to different legal standards than demands for use of existing track.

Cases involving telegraph lines strung along railroad rights of way established important precedents. The technologies were symbiotic in that the railroads used the telegraph to communicate train locations, and they were usually willing to allow telegraph companies to erect poles alongside tracks in exchange for providing free telegraph service to the railroad. Disagreements did arise, however, typically when more than one telegraph company sought to string wires on a railroad's right of way. Telegraph cases were cited in later cases allowing a second railroad to condemn certain property of an existing railroad in order to lay its own track alongside, even though the two railroads would be competing with one another.

One telegraph case established an important caveat to the rule that the public has an interest in railroad rights of way. Upon expiration of a contract agreement between a railroad and a telegraph company, the railroad decided to contract with a competing telegraph firm and to eject the incumbent telegraph company from the right of way, disposing of its poles and wires.[44] The incumbent company argued that railroads were public highways and hence subject to occupation under an 1866 statute that gave telegraph companies the right to the "public domain."[45] The Supreme Court disagreed, stating, "A railroad's right of way is property devoted to a public use and has often been called a highway, and as such is subject, to a certain extent, to state and Federal control but it is so far private property as to be entitled to the protection of the Constitution so that it can only be taken under the power of eminent domain ... or with the consent of the railroad."

A second telegraph precedent relevant to passenger access to freight track turned on whether use of the right of way would interfere with the railroad's operations.[46] The Illinois Supreme Court ruled that a railroad wishing to start its own telegraph service could not prevent the incumbent telegraph company from condemning its right of way and maintaining its poles and wires on railroad property, because stringing an additional wire between the existing telegraph poles would cause no additional interference with the railroad's operations.

The principle of no material interference established in the telegraph cases was also applied to unused, unimportant, or superfluous railroad property. During the boom years of railroad construction at the turn of the last century, available rights of way were lacking for subsequent railroads in some built-up areas. These railroads sought to condemn portions of existing rights of way. Citing the telegraph cases, the North Carolina Supreme Court allowed a competing railroad serving Charlotte to condemn a portion of another railroad's right of way for a few hundred feet through the city.[47] A similar ruling was issued regarding two railroads in Danbury, CT, where the owning railroad had graded right of way wide enough for two parallel tracks but had only laid one track.[48] Because this land was not being used, the court allowed it to be condemned by another railroad. The court noted the public's interest in having tracks not take up more land than necessary, as well as the economy of two railroads sharing the cost of maintaining a roadbed.

In Washington State, a railroad was able to condemn 28 feet of an existing railroad's 100-foot-wide right of way for a distance of several hundred feet because the owning railroad was not making use of a portion of its right of way.[49] The state court cited a provision in the state's property law authorizing condemnation not only of roadbed but also of track, implying that in certain circumstances two railroads could be required to operate trains over the same track. The two rail carriers would share a common easement over the track.

ABANDONMENTS, DISCONTINUANCES, PROFITABILITY: DOES IT PROVIDE A BASIS FOR PASSENGER ACCESS TO FREIGHT TRACKS?

If the Surface Transportation Board were to be empowered as an arbitrator for passenger access to freight facilities, a related question is how the board could balance the needs of the competing interests. How could the public's need for passenger service be measured? Must it be vital or merely convenient? Could a freight railroad be forced to forego some amount of freight revenue in order to make room for passenger trains? If so, how much forgone revenue is tolerable? Should a prosperous railroad be required to forego more revenue than a financially weak railroad? The Interstate Commerce Commission, the STB, and the courts have usually addressed these questions in the context of permitting railroads to discontinue a service, but their responses may shed light on how the railroads' public service obligations might be weighed in the face of demands for an additional service.

After World War I, passenger rail service went through a period of contraction followed by stagnation. Intercity bus and automobile travel began to attract passengers away from trains. The Great Depression made matters much worse; many major railroads entered bankruptcy. An ICC study conducted in the late 1950s cited 1930 as the first year that the industry ran an operating deficit from passenger service.[50] This deficit increased year after year, except during World War II.

Beginning with the Transportation Act of 1920 (P.L. 66-152, 41 Stat. 456), which returned the railroads to the private sector after nationalization during World War I, Congress demonstrated increasing concern with the financial health of the carriers. Congress recognized that the system was too large in scope and operated by too many carriers for optimal performance on a national scale. The 1920 act included a number of provisions aimed at consolidating the nation's railroads. One of these provisions allowed the railroads to petition the ICC to abandon unprofitable lines. Prior to the 1920 act, states had been an obstacle to abandonment, often requiring railroads to continue providing local services at a loss. The terms by which the ICC was to evaluate abandonments became the basis for it to evaluate proposed passenger service discontinuances after World War II: the law required the ICC to weigh "public convenience and necessity" and the financial health of the railroad. Between 1920 and 1963, the ICC permitted the abandonment of nearly 50,000 miles of railroad, approximately one-fifth of the total mileage that existed in

1920.[51] It is not known how much of this mileage, if the right of way was still clear, would be useful today for passenger service.

The Transportation Act of 1920 addressed only total abandonment of a line, and did not give the ICC authority to regulate railroads' attempts to discontinue just the passenger trains over a line while continuing freight train service. This shortcoming was highlighted by a case in which a railroad appealed to the Wisconsin Public Service Commission to cancel passenger train service on a 27-mile line only during the winter months due to light traffic. The Wisconsin commission refused, and later denied the railroad's petition to replace rail service with bus service during the winter months. The railroad then filed an abandonment petition with the ICC. The ICC allowed the abandonment, which meant the discontinuance of freight service and summer passenger service as well.[52] Thus, federal authority over abandonments had an "all or nothing" aspect to it.

In the Transportation Act of 1958 (P.L. 85-625, 72 Stat. 571), Congress granted the ICC authority to allow a railroad to discontinue passenger service over a line while continuing freight service.[53] For *intra*state passenger service, a railroad was required to first petition its state government. If the state prohibited discontinuance, the railroad could then appeal to the ICC. For *inter*state passenger routes, a railroad could discontinue the service but it would be subject to a stay by the ICC.[54] The ICC had four months to decide if it should stay (delay) the service discontinuance, which it could only do for one year.

One passenger train discontinuance case reached the Supreme Court in 1964.[55] The Southern Railway sought to discontinue the last two passenger trains between Greensboro and Goldsboro, NC. The ICC granted the discontinuance on the grounds that the cost of providing the passenger service was three times the revenue it produced and that the need for the service was insubstantial. The federal district court overturned the ICC ruling,[56] but the Supreme Court, with two Justices dissenting, reinstated it. The Supreme Court majority opinion held that where the demands of public convenience and necessity are slight, as in this case, it was proper for the ICC in determining the existence of a burden on interstate commerce to give little weight to the carrier's overall prosperity. In its argument, the majority also referred to the opposite situation, citing the example of unprofitable commuter trains. The majority stated that in cases involving "vital commuter services in large metropolitan areas where the demands of public convenience and necessity are large, it is of course obvious that the Commission would err if it did not give great weight to the ability of the carrier to absorb even large deficits resulting from such services."

The two dissenting Justices asserted that if railroads were allowed to terminate service based solely on the availability of alternate modes of transportation and a finding of a "net loss" on the service, railroads would discontinue virtually all of their commuter trains. The dissenters cited a 1958 Supreme Court case that upheld the principle that a railroad that was prosperous overall could be required to provide particular services at a loss.[57] The 1958 case involved the Chicago, Milwaukee, St. Paul & Pacific Railroad, which appealed to the Illinois Commerce Commission to raise commuter fares so as to avoid a yearly loss of over $300,000. The Illinois commission denied the fare raise. The railroad appealed to the ICC, which granted enough of a fare increase for the railroad to break even on the commuter service. However, the Supreme Court ruled against the ICC and in favor of the Illinois commission, criticizing the ICC for not giving due consideration to the overall profitability of the railroad's operations in Illinois.

The 1958 and 1964 Supreme Court cases suggest that where passenger service is deemed vital, a profitable railroad could in some circumstances be required to provide such service even at a loss. These precedents raise an important question regarding the terms of passenger access to freight track in the present day. Can a freight railroad be required to provide passenger operators access to its facilities at less than what it perceives as the full market value?

When Congress directed the ICC to balance public convenience and necessity with the burden on interstate commerce in considering railroads' requests to abandon track or discontinue passenger service, it did not indicate how heavy a burden was acceptable. The ICC generally equated "public convenience and necessity" with passenger interests. However, in a 1965 case that allowed the Boston and Main Railroad to discontinue two passenger trains, the ICC defined the public interest to include the shipping customers of the railroad. The ICC concluded that in order to preserve the railroad for freight customers, passenger service must be permitted to end.[58]

Government Takeover of Passenger Service

The stakes became higher as the railroad industry's financial situation deteriorated in the 1960s. Railroads began approaching the ICC with wholesale requests to discontinue all of their passenger trains. For instance, in

1966 the trustees running the New York, New Haven, and Hartford Railroad filed to discontinue all of the railroad's 278 interstate passenger trains, including commuter trains for New York, Boston, and Providence, as well as intercity trains. These trains made 1,244 trips in a typical week and carried 76 million passengers in 1964.[59] This railroad's passenger service was deemed as important, if not more so, than its freight service. The ICC blocked the discontinuance of all but a few of the passenger trains.[60]

In 1970, Penn Central petitioned the ICC to discontinue 34 passenger trains, including all of the railroad's east-west intercity passenger service west of Buffalo, NY, and Harrisburg, PA. This petition, which would have ended passenger rail service between New York and Chicago, gave momentum to legislation creating a national passenger railroad corporation.

The discontinuance of privately provided commuter train service led to public ownership of these services. The Long Island Railroad, while the busiest commuter railroad in the country, nevertheless did not have sufficient freight traffic to cover its losses on passenger service. It was the first commuter line to fall into public ownership, in 1966.

Discontinuance of service also led to federal subsidization of commuter operations. The mayors of large cities with commuter operations were alarmed when railroads proposed their discontinuance and sought assistance from the federal government. Federal assistance began in the early 1960s and included assistance to private entities, but under the Urban Mass Transportation Act of 1964, federal funding for transit could only be granted to public entities, thus encouraging the public takeover of privately owned commuter services. For example, the Massachusetts Bay Transportation Authority was formed in 1964 to subsidize commuter lines, finally purchasing many lines from the railroads in the 1970s. The city of Philadelphia began subsidizing commuter service in 1958 and, with cooperation from surrounding counties, formed a regional authority in the 1960s to consolidate governance of commuter operations. New Jersey began subsidizing commuter trains in 1964, began buying new rolling stock for private operators in 1968, and eventually created New Jersey Transit in 1982.

The Creation of Rights for Passenger Train Access

The petition of the Penn Central Railroad to discontinue intercity passenger service in the Northeast and Midwest gave momentum to passage of the Rail Passenger Service Act of 1970 (P.L. 91-518), the law that created

Amtrak. Amtrak was established as a mixed corporation; it was set up as a private corporation but all its common stock was owned by U.S. taxpayers and its preferred stock would be owned by participating railroads. Amtrak was to take over intercity (but not commuter) passenger service from those railroads choosing to turn the service over to Amtrak. Each railroad was required to pay Amtrak an amount based on the railroad's losses from passenger service in 1969. If Amtrak was not able to reach an agreement with a railroad for use of its tracks or other facilities, the ICC was authorized to order the railroad to make its assets available to Amtrak and to set just and reasonable terms and compensation for their use.[61]

In 1973, Congress amended the 1970 act to augment Amtrak's bargaining power with the freight railroads. It required freight railroads to give "preference" to Amtrak trains operating on their track (i.e., they are supposed to be given priority over freight trains when dispatching trains), authorized Amtrak to buy rights of way and stations or acquire them by eminent domain, set Amtrak's compensation to freight railroads for use of their track at incremental costs (thus not contributing to fixed and overhead costs), and allowed Amtrak to appeal to the U.S. Department of Transportation in the event that a freight railroad refused to allow higher-speed trains on its track.[62] Since passage of the 1970 amendments, freight railroads have contended they subsidize Amtrak service because Amtrak pays only the freight railroads' additional cost of running Amtrak trains without contributing to fixed and overhead costs. Thus, some freight railroads continue to have a form of passenger service obligation by carrying Amtrak trains at what they view as a subsidized price.

The shrinkage of the rail network in the 1970s and 1980s provided, at least potentially, opportunities to use abandoned freight lines for passenger service, facilitated by important statutory and regulatory changes to the abandonment process discussed below. In 1972, the ICC attempted to simplify the abandonment process by adopting a rule that, with a rebuttable presumption, it would probably grant an automatic abandonment (without a hearing) if a line annually averaged less than 34 cars per mile.[63] Between 1970 and 1976, 15,000 miles of railroads were abandoned.[64]

Access via the "Forced-Sale" Provision

In 1980, with passage of the Staggers Act (P.L. 96-448), Congress required that, if a responsible party came forward offering to buy or subsidize a line slated for abandonment, the line could not be abandoned and the ICC would set the terms and the conditions for purchase of the line. This so-called "forced sale" provision proved very useful for would-be passenger operators, particularly local authorities seeking to provide commuter rail or mass transit service, as a freight railroad was more likely to be flexible in bargaining knowing that if there were no agreement on a sale price, the ICC would set the price and terms of sale.[65]

The "forced-sale" provision was used in 1981 by a commuter agency in the Chicago suburbs to acquire a 17-mile section of track that the Chicago and North Western (C&NW) Railroad had slated for abandonment. The price set by the ICC was much closer to the offer made by the commuter agency than the offer made by the C&NW Railroad.[66] This illustrates why many commuter operators favor having Amtrak-like legal powers to negotiate access to freight railroads, as those powers reduce freight railroads' leverage in bargaining.

Access via "Adverse Abandonment"

Another important ICC case from the same period established the precedent of "adverse abandonment." If another entity, such as a passenger rail authority or shipper group, wishes to restore rail service over a dormant rail line that the owning railroad is not planning to abandon, that party could appeal to the ICC to force abandonment by the owning railroad. This precedent was set by a Kansas City-area transit authority that sought to use a fallow rail corridor.[67] The transit authority first tried to condemn the property, but the court disallowed the condemnation because the ICC had not issued an abandonment certificate, meaning that the line was still part of the national rail network and under the ICC's jurisdiction, preempting the condemnation proceeding. The transit authority then petitioned the ICC to issue an abandonment certificate over the owning railroad's objection. The ICC did so because the owning railroad had not provided rail service nor conducted any maintenance work on the line in over a decade and was making no efforts to solicit customers on the line.

Rail-Banking

Congress's concern with the extent of abandonments led to passage in 1983 of amendments to the National Trails System Act (P.L. 98-11). These amendments allowed railroad rights of way to be preserved for interim recreational trail use or for telecommunication facilities, retaining a railroad's right to reactivate a rail line if future needs dictated. Congress had expressed this intent also in the 1976 4-R Act (§809 of P.L. 94-210), but the language in that act had failed to produce the desired result. The process in the 4-R Act had included as an initial step before rail-banking that the line in question be officially granted an abandonment certificate. Upon this designation, however, abutting property owners claimed rights of ownership to the right of way land.[68]

Amtrak Uses Its Eminent Domain Power

In 1987, Amtrak discontinued its service to Montreal because a 49-mile section of track between Brattleboro and Windsor, VT, was not adequately maintained by the owning railroad. Amtrak believed a 1977 contract entitled it to operate its trains at 60 miles per hour, but the track condition only satisfied the host freight railroad's need for 25 mile-per-hour train speeds. When negotiations broke down, Amtrak turned to the nearby competitor of the host shortline railroad. The competitor and Amtrak entered into an agreement in which Amtrak would use its eminent domain power to acquire the segment of track (via an application to the ICC). Amtrak would immediately sell the track to the competitor, and would pay the competitor an agreed-upon price for track maintenance.

In a series of decisions, the ICC approved the condemnation, after which Amtrak and the competitor executed their agreements, the track was upgraded, and Amtrak resumed its service to Montreal in July 1989. The ICC chairman dissented from the majority decision, stating that it would be "hard to imagine a more blatant misuse of the public's eminent domain power," and also argued that neither Amtrak nor the ICC had the power to restructure the competitive relationship between the two shortlines.[69] The U.S. Court of Appeals for the D.C. Circuit overturned the ICC decision,[70] holding that Amtrak did not have authority to condemn property for the purpose of selling it to another railroad. Congress then amended the statute specifically to authorize this type of condemnation. The D.C. Circuit denied a rehearing,[71] but its original decision was reversed by the Supreme Court.[72] This is the only case in which Amtrak has resorted to its eminent domain power when dealing with what it perceives to be an intransigent freight railroad.

Running passenger trains on a host freight railroad track inevitably involves cooperation on a daily basis. Negotiations are not over once the terms of access are agreed upon. Intervention by a federal regulator—responsibility for Amtrak's access to freight track now rests with the Surface Transportation Board—might poison the relationship between passenger operator and host railroad, inhibiting the cooperation necessary to provide good service. Indeed, several years later Amtrak faced resistance from the parent company of the same railroad in trying to increase speeds on a 78-mile section of track between Portland, ME, and Plaistow, NH, for its "Downeaster" service to

Boston.[73] Some commuter authorities have not sought government intervention in disputes out of concern that this would complicate future relations with host railroads.[74]

The Common Carrier Obligation Fades

When it passed the Staggers Act of 1980 to deregulate the rail industry, Congress maintained railroads' common carrier obligation. The act allowed railroads and shippers, for the first time, to enter into confidential contracts with one another, but it specified that these contracts could not impair a railroad's ability to meet its common carrier obligations. However, the overall thrust of the Staggers Act was to allow railroads more leeway to make decisions based on their economic interests. An important development indicating the extent to which railroads are now able to act like any other business is the treatment of opportunity costs.

Opportunity cost is the economic loss experienced by a carrier from foregoing a more profitable alternative use of its assets. In terms of potentially tipping the scale between private and public interests in railroads, opportunity cost is a weighty matter. The ICC struggled with whether it was appropriate to consider opportunity costs in rail line abandonment proceedings, and amended its balancing test in 1980 to allow a railroad to abandon a line if it could show that the resources tied up in owning and maintaining it could earn a higher return elsewhere.[75]

Allowing freight railroads to cite opportunity costs as a basis for limiting their public service obligations potentially establishes a high economic hurdle for passenger train operators demanding access to freight railroad facilities. A freight railroad could claim that resources (such as track capacity) it would have to devote to passenger trains could achieve a higher return if used to expand freight service. This argument may be particularly powerful if there is no spare capacity.

PASSENGER ACCESS IN AN ERA OF TIGHT CAPACITY

Since railroad deregulation in 1980, the supply and demand for freight railroad facilities has come closer to equilibrium. What Congress set out to achieve in the Transportation Act of 1920, consolidation and the shedding of excess capacity, has been largely achieved. Since 2004, the Surface

Transportation Board has required each railroad to submit a plan each year describing how it intends to avoid capacity shortages during the grain harvest season. Many railroads have been investing heavily to increase capacity, including, in some cases, restoring sections of double track in locations where the second track had been removed many years ago.

The disappearance of excess capacity was related to the decline of passenger service. Supporting passenger train operations had led many railroads to install multiple tracks, yard bypasses, and sophisticated signaling systems. This infrastructure generated additional capacity by allowing trains of varying speeds to use the same rights of way. Without passenger trains, the freight railroads could shed much of this capacity and could also economize by maintaining tracks for freight-train speeds rather than for the higher speeds needed for competitive passenger service.[76]

Tighter supply of rail facilities has raised questions about the railroads' public obligations in such an environment. Under such conditions, what is a reasonable request for rail service? Does a railroad have an obligation to expand capacity in order to meet additional requests for service? As stated in one Supreme Court case, "the common law of old in requiring the carrier to receive all goods and passengers recognized that 'if his coach be full' he was not liable for failing to transport more than he could carry."[77] Without enough room to accommodate everyone, a carrier still must treat customers fairly, if not identically.[78]

What it means to treat customers fairly is complicated by the unique demands of passenger service. Passenger trains typically operate at higher speeds than freight trains, and railroads insist that a mix of speeds on the same track can actually reduce the number of trains that can be operated. Further, while some freight trains operate on tight schedules, many do not, and a passenger operator's insistence upon on-time performance may cause conflict with less time-sensitive freight operations.

Public Authorities Avoid Acquiring Common Carrier Status

An earlier section discussed how public authorities could acquire railroad rights of way that had been officially abandoned. Upon issuing a certificate of abandonment, the ICC (now the STB) no longer has jurisdiction over the right of way. Thus, if a public authority were to acquire an officially abandoned line, the STB (the ICC's successor) would not have jurisdiction over the authority because it would not be deemed a "rail carrier" as defined in statute, nor would the "common carrier obligation" (potentially requiring the authority to provide freight rail service upon reasonable request) be attached to the authority. However, if a state or local agency wished to acquire a non-abandoned rail line from a freight railroad willing to sell, the agency would acquire the status of a common carrier along with the obligation that this status entails.

In 1991, the ICC issued a ruling that has allowed public rail authorities to acquire active freight lines without acquiring the common carrier status, which has greatly facilitated public takeover of lines for passenger use. The ICC ruling involved a 16-mile rail segment owned by the Maine Central Railroad which the state of Maine wanted to purchase for use in a new passenger rail service. The transaction was structured so that the freight railroad retained a permanent, exclusive easement to carry freight over the line.[79] Thus, the freight railroad retained its common carrier obligation over the line, not encumbering the state of Maine with this obligation. This transaction has since served as precedent for numerous access transactions (more than 60 cases). It allows a state or local government to provide rail passenger service without acquiring the status of a common carrier.[80]

In these transactions, the STB has attempted to facilitate passenger use of the right of way while at the same time protecting the common carrier obligation attached to the line. The STB has allowed operating agreements between freight railroads and passenger operators to restrict freight operations to specific parts of the day and has allowed passenger operators to assume responsibility for maintenance and dispatching over lines also used for freight. However, the STB has disapproved of transactions in which the passenger operator would have gained so much control over the line that it could have thwarted enforcement of the common carrier obligation.

Separating the physical assets from an operating easement over a railroad line raises an important but unresolved question. Could a public authority forcibly acquire a mere passenger easement or some other partial condemnation of a freight line for the purposes of providing passenger service over the line? A freight railroad right of way could be wide enough that condemning only a portion of the right of way for adding parallel track would not interfere with freight operations. Similarly, acquiring an easement for only certain times of the day may not interfere with freight operations. In so doing, it is possible that this partial condemnation would not be judged by the courts/STB to interfere with interstate commerce and therefore permissible.[81]

Passenger Access via the Track-Sharing Provision

The Transportation Act of 1920 included a provision under which the ICC could require railroads to share terminal facilities including main-line track for a reasonable distance outside the terminal.[82] This provision has survived as current law, in amended form but with no substantive changes. It is currently codified at 49 U.S.C. 11102(a):

> The Board may require terminal facilities, including main-line tracks for a reasonable distance outside of a terminal, owned by a rail carrier providing transportation subject to the jurisdiction of the Board under this part, to be used by another rail carrier if the Board finds that use to be practicable and in the public interest without substantially impairing the ability of the rail carrier owning the facilities or entitled to use the facilities to handle its own business. The rail carriers are responsible for establishing the conditions and compensation for use of the facilities. However, if the rail carriers cannot agree, the Board may establish conditions and compensation for use of the facilities under the principle controlling compensation in condemnation proceedings. The compensation shall be paid or adequately secured before a rail carrier may begin to use the facilities of another rail carrier under this section.

This provision has been a focus of competitive access disputes between railroads and some of their "singularly served" customers, but was not considered in the context of passenger access to freight facilities until the 1990s. In 1991, a Southern California commuter rail authority, citing this provision, appealed to the ICC to break an impasse between it and a freight railroad over its use of freight track.[83] In 1998, the provision was used again by commuter interests in the same region when unable to reach agreement with a freight railroad for use of its right of way.[84] In both cases, the commuter authorities eventually reached agreements with the freight railroads without ICC/STB intervention, so the legality of using this provision for access by passenger operators has not been tested in court. One question is whether a public agency that is not yet engaged in rail transportation would qualify as "another rail carrier," as required in the statute.[85]

CONGRESS EXTINGUISHES RESIDUAL
LOCAL REGULATION

Fifteen years after deregulating the transportation system, Congress abolished the ICC and replaced it with the STB in the ICC Termination Act of 1995 (ICCTA, P.L. 104-88, 109 Stat. 830). ICCTA kept in place the deregulatory framework of the Staggers Act. One modification made in ICCTA, however, has had a profound impact on a state's or municipality's prospects for gaining access to freight rights of way—perhaps shutting the door on the possibility except on terms acceptable to the freight railroad.

Prior to ICCTA, the federal government and the states had some concurrent jurisdiction over railroad rates, classifications, rules, and practices, and states and localities retained authority over the construction, acquisition, operation, abandonment, or discontinuance of spur, industrial, team, switching, or side tracks if the tracks were located, or intended to be located, entirely in one state. Under ICCTA, these aspects of rail regulation were placed under the exclusive jurisdiction of the STB.[86] As stated in the House report, this change was made "to reflect the direct and complete preemption of State economic regulation of railroads."[87]

This change consolidating jurisdiction under the federal government has been cited by the STB and the courts when blocking state or local government attempts to condemn portions of railroad rights-of-way for other public purposes. As discussed above, prior to ICCTA it may have been possible for local governments to condemn railroad property for some other public use if the second use would not materially interfere with railroad operations.[88] Court decisions in condemnation cases since ICCTA indicate this is no longer the case. For instance, a Wisconsin city, citing its authority under its police power, attempted to condemn a portion of a railroad's right of way used for passing track in order to straighten an unsafe curve in a road parallel to the railroad.[89] The court ruled that the city could not condemn the railroad property because condemnation would be a form of rail regulation, preempted by ICCTA. Similarly, the city of Lincoln, NE was unable to condemn a 20-foot-wide strip of railroad right of way for a distance of five blocks for use as a pedestrian and bike trail.[90] The railroad contended that it was using this property for loading and unloading lumber and that trail users would be too close to the tracks, creating a safety hazard. The STB sided with the railroad, finding the proposed taking would unduly interfere with interstate commerce. In another case, the city of St. Paul, MN, sought to condemn a 24-foot-wide strip of railroad right of way for about 2 miles for use as a bike trail.[91] A federal court held that the issue of potential interference with railroad operations was not even relevant because the condemnation action in and of itself triggered the ICCTA preemption.

These cases, at the turn of this century, could be viewed as the other bookend to the station stoppage cases at the turn of the last century. Recall that the prevailing argument for upholding community stoppage laws back then was that local governments, rather than a "distant authority," could "more wisely" and with "deeper concern" manage the rights of way in their jurisdictions.

The same ICCTA provision appears to block attempts by passenger carriers seeking to gain access to freight rights of way at a lower price through condemnation rather than paying a negotiated price. In 2006, the Chicago Transit Authority sought to condemn a 2.8 mile-long right of way over which it ran two tracks alongside the three tracks of the Union Pacific Railroad. The transit authority had leased the land from Union Pacific for 50 years. In negotiations over lease renewal, the parties were unable to reach an agreement on the rent, and when the freight railroad rejected the transit authority's proposal for a one-time payment, the transit authority began a condemnation proceeding. The court found that ICCTA preempted the condemnation proceeding, again because condemnation was a form of local regulation barred by the law.[92]

OPTIONS FOR CONGRESS

From a freight railroad's perspective, an important distinction is whether allowing passenger trains would absorb otherwise idle capacity or would displace revenue freight trains. Freight railroads expect commuter rail authorities to pay for freight revenues foregone due to use of capacity for passenger service, and there is often disagreement over how severely the passenger operations compromise the railroad's ability to run additional freight trains.[93] Congress might consider whether the Federal Railroad Administration, experts in determining the infrastructure requirements for safe operation, could provide an independent assessment.

To passenger rail proponents, disputes over access to a limited track network are indicative of a lack of federal investment in this mode. Double tracking a rail network that is largely "stuck in a one-track world"[94] would be one, albeit an expensive, option for reducing conflicts between freight and passenger use of track. The transcontinental freight railroads have, in recent years, been adding parallel tracks on their busiest routes. Shorter-haul intermodal, refrigerated, and parcel cargoes are an incentive for freight railroads to provide "express" services, perhaps requiring additional parallel track along segments of their networks. Yet, one of their largest express customers, UPS, has voiced frustration with the slow pace of their investment, including their slow pace in adopting new technology, like positive train control, that could increase capacity.[95] Freight railroads and "higher"-speed intercity passenger operators (as opposed to "high-speed" trains operating on dedicated passenger track) could potentially share an interest in express track construction. One method that has been proposed as a public-private partnership in enhancing rail infrastructure is the creation of a federal rail trust fund, financed by taxes on the users of the system.[96]

UPS's rail service needs raise a fundamental question for Congress. Can the same rail network be expected to satisfy the needs of both shippers and passengers? UPS, like many shippers, requires a fluid rail network from coast to coast, with trains arriving reliably on time and in sync with its tightly "choreographed" logistics network. Is this possible if a transcontinental UPS train must be shunted to a siding every time it encounters an Amtrak train, or each time it approaches a city along the way during rush hour?[97]

Given the increasing demands on urban rail corridors, Congress may wish to consider alternatives for managing them. The "port authority" model might help manage some of the competing uses.[98] Similar to a seaport authority, a publicly owned "rail port authority" could purchase key rail corridors (many marine terminals were once owned by railroads) in order to rationalize, reconfigure, or otherwise improve a city's rail network for both passenger and freight use. While freight railroads can be expected to maximize use of their individual rights of way, as rivals they have little incentive to analyze an urban rail system as a whole or minimize conflicts with intersecting roadways. Similar to the municipal takeover of commuter services, publicly owned freight rail facilities would become eligible for a broader array of federal transportation funding programs. Public funding could help such authorities amass a level of capital that the private railroads are unable or unwilling to provide. Railroads using the facility would have to pay fees, which they may find agreeable because they avoid the need for large, upfront capital outlays.

A similar model has been used by the Alameda Corridor Transportation Authority in Southern California, which purchased and modernized a freight rail line linking the ports with inland terminals. Grade separating this 20-mile rail corridor through the city increased freight train speeds, eliminated grade crossing conflicts, and freed up capacity on three other rail lines through the city. The freight railroads pay fees to the authority to run trains over the corridor. While the Alameda Corridor is not used for passenger service, this type of structure could address the concern that implementing passenger service on one railroad's corridor could disrupt the competitive balance between competing freight carriers.

The option of gaining access via purchase of freight rights of way by a public rail authority returns the discussion to the price of that access. Thus, the fundamental issue is whether freight railroads and prospective passenger rail authorities should negotiate over the price of railroad property just as any private parties would or whether an independent, but governmental, third party, such as the STB, should have some role in determining the terms of sale. Some railroad rights of way have been purchased by passenger rail operators through normal market negotiations, and thus one could conclude that the marketplace is capable of determining their relative value, in terms of passenger or freight use. However, two aspects of these transactions make them different than the typical private property sale. For one, there is only one potential buyer and only one potential seller. Second, public authorities are not seeking access to railroad rights of way to use them for some non-rail public purpose, merely to use them for their intended purpose. Neither are public authorities asking the freight railroads to absorb the losses of operating passenger trains, as they once were required to. The risk of losses remains with the public. Given that a public service obligation is still attached to railroads, albeit largely lifted with respect to passenger service, do freight railroads have the right to solely set the price for passenger access or should the public's convenience and necessity be given some consideration?

A following question is who should be granted a legal right to insist upon use of freight track for passenger service? Congress might limit that right to Amtrak, as under present law, but could also extend it to agencies of state and local governments, such as transit authorities. Creating track access rights for potential private operators of rail service may be a particularly thorny issue. Congress has indicated a desire to promote private investment in intercity passenger rail service, but potential private competitors to Amtrak may expect the same privileged access to freight track that Amtrak enjoys.

End Notes

[1] The STB, successor agency to the Interstate Commerce Commission (ICC), is bi-partisan, independent, and organizationally housed within the U.S. Department of Transportation (DOT). It has economic regulatory jurisdiction over freight railroad mergers, abandonments, new construction, and, under certain circumstances, the reasonableness of rates charged for providing rail transportation services.

[2] By statue, Amtrak must pay railroads that host Amtrak trains the incremental cost imposed, but need not contribute to the recovery of fixed costs or overhead costs.

[3] This is not to say that state or local officials would not have any political leverage when negotiating with freight railroads.

[4] This option is supported by many, but not all, commuter rail authorities. See *Commuter Rail: Information and Guidance Could Help Facilitate Commuter and Freight Rail Access Negotiations,* January 2004, GAO-04-240, p. 32. Some states pursuing high speed intercity passenger rail projects also support this option, see written testimony of John D. Porcari, Deputy Secretary, U.S. Department of Transportation, Senate Committee on Commerce, Science, and Transportation, hearing on The Federal Role in National Transportation Policy, September 15, 2010, p. 5. A bill (H.R. 2654, the TRAIN Act) that would authorize the federal Surface Transportation Board (STB) to act as an arbitrator between freight and commuter rail operators, as it does for Amtrak and freight railroads, was introduced but received no committee action in the 107th Congress.

[5] Letters from Union Pacific Railroad to California High-Speed Rail Authority dated May 13, 2008 and April 23, 2010. See also "High-Speed Rail Stalls; Freight Carriers Balk at Sharing Tracks With the Faster Passenger Service," *Wall Street Journal* (Online) September 21, 2010.

[6] "High-Speed Rail Money on Hold," *Albany Times Union,* August 4, 2011, p. C-1.

[7] "RTD May Take 90 Homes if Light-Rail Option Picked," *Denver Post,* October 2, 2006, p. B-5.

[8] "Transit Pitch Meets Rancor," *Denver Post,* March 6, 2012, p. A-1.

[9] "De-Railed; As Rail Business Booms, Giant CSX Has Frustrated Local Officials In Their Efforts To Acquire Tracks for Commuter Rail, Bike Trails," *Boston Globe,* October 21, 2007, p. 1. "Stalemate on Commuter Rail Tied to CSX," *Boston Globe*, March 23, 2008, p. GW-1.

[10] "CSX, Florida Close Commuter Rail Deal," *Transport Topics,* Nov. 14, 2011, p. 14.

[11] Paul Stephen Dempsey, "Transportation: A Legal History," *Transportation Law Journal,* v. 30, no. 2-3, Spring-Summer 2003.

[12] Carter Goodrich, *Government Promotion of American Canals and Railroads 1800-1890,* Columbia Univ. Press, New York, 1960.

[13] The Commutation Rate Case, 21 ICC 428 (1911).

[14] James W. Ely, Jr., *Railroads and American Law,* Univ. Press of Kansas, 2001, p. 7.

[15] Jurgen Basedow, "Common Carriers, Continuity and Disintegration in U.S. Transportation Law," *Transportation Law Journal,* vol. 13, 1983-1984, pp. 1-188.

[16] *Bloodgood v. The Mohawk and Hudson Railroad Co.,* 18 Wendell (N.Y.) 9, 1837 N.Y. Lexis 137.

[17] Paul Stephen Dempsey, "Transportation: A Legal History," *Transportation Law Journal,* v. 30, no. 2-3, Spring-Summer 2003, p. 299.

[18] *Munn v. Illinois,* 94 U.S. 113 (1876). Although this case did not directly involve railroads (Munn was a grain elevator company), subsequent cases applied this principle to railroads.

[19] *Munn v. Illinois,* 94 U.S. 143 (1876).

[20] 118 U.S. 557 (1886).

[21] Act to Regulate Commerce, Ch. 104, 24 Stat. 379 (1887).

[22] *Chicago, Milwaukee and St. Paul Railway v. Minnesota,* 134 U.S. 418 (1890).

[23] James W. Ely, Jr. "The Railroad Question Revisited: Chicago, Milwaukee and St. Paul Railway v. Minnesota and Constitutional Limits on State Regulations," *Great Plains Quarterly,* Spring 1992, pp. 121-134.

[24] *Houston, East and West Texas Railway Co. v. United States,* 234 U.S. 342 (1914).

[25] William E. Thoms, "Regulation of Passenger Train Discontinuances," *Journal of Public Law,* v. 22, 1973, p. 105.

[26] 34 Stat. 584.

[27] The cases cited in this section draw heavily upon those discussed in James W. Ely, Jr., "The Railroad System Has Burst Through State Limits: Railroads and Interstate Commerce, 1830-1920," *Arkansas Law Review,* v. 55, 2002-2003, pp. 933-980.

[28] 163 U.S. 142 (1896).

[29] 218 U.S. 135 (1910).

[30] *Gladstone v. Minnesota,* 166 U.S. 427 (1897).

[31] *Lake Shore & Michigan Southern Railway Co. v. Ohio,* 173 U.S. 285 (1899).

[32] 173 U.S. 285 (1899); 1899 U.S. LEXIS 1438, p. 9.

[33] For examples of conflicts over this distinction today, see Maureen E. Eldredge, "Who's Driving the Train? Railroad Regulation and Local Control," *University of Colorado Law Review,* v. 75, Spring 2004, pp. 549-595.

[34] Raising overhead clearances can also improve the efficiency of passenger trains by allowing for double-deck cars.

[35] See Massachusetts Dept. of Transportation—Acquisition Exemption—Certain Assets of CSX Transportation, STB Docket No. FD35312, May 3, 2010 and the discussion under "Public Authorities Avoid Acquiring Common Carrier Status."

[36] See http://www.createprogram.org/.

[37] See http://www.edrgroup.com/library/freight/rail-freight-futures-for-the-city-of-chicago.html.

[38] *Escanaba Co. v. Chicago,* 107 U.S. 678 (1882).

[39] 203 U.S. 335 (1906).

[40] 203 U.S. 335, 346.

[41] See Testimony of Richard F. Timmons, President of the American Short Line and Regional Railroad Association, STB Ex Parte No. 677, Hearing on the Common Carrier Obligation, April 25, 2008.

[42] Since 1920, the average length of haul for a rail freight shipment has increased from 327 miles to over 900 miles. Association of American Railroads, *Railroad Facts,* 2009 edition.

[43] DOT IG, *Root Causes of Amtrak Train Delays,* September 8, 2008, report no. CR-2008-076, p. 15. See also, Jeremy Grant, "Ageing U.S. Rail Networks Stuck in a One-Track World," *Financial Times,* September 13, 2004.

[44] *Western Union Telegraph Co. v. Pennsylvania Railroad Co. et al.,* 195 U.S. 540 (1904).

[45] The Act of Congress of July 24, 1866 (14 Stat. 221).

[46] *The Western Union Telegraph Co. of Illinois v. The Louisville and Nashville Railroad Co.,* 270 Ill. 399 (1915).

[47] *North Carolina and Richmond and Danville Railroad Co. v. Carolina Central Railway Co. and others.,* 83 N.C. 489 (1880).

[48] *The New York Housatonic & Northern Railroad Co. v. The Boston, Hartford, and Erie Railroad Co.,* 36 Conn. 196 (1869).

[49] *Seattle and Montana Railroad Co. v. Bellingham Bay and Eastern Railroad Co.,* 29 Wash. 491 (1902).

[50] ICC, *Railroad Passenger Train Deficit,* 306 ICC 417 (1959).

[51] Steven R. Wild, "A History of Railroad Abandonments," *Transportation Law Journal,* v. 23, 1995-1996.

[52] 295 ICC 157, 1956.

[53] The 1958 Act provision regarding passenger service discontinuance may have been prompted specifically by the New York Central Railroad, which wished to discontinue passenger ferry service across the Hudson River but not its freight ferry service (see 372 U.S. 1, 5-6).

[54] This arrangement was a result of a compromise between the Senate version, which would have allowed a railroad to petition the ICC directly for both intra- and interstate services, and the House version which would not have given the ICC any jurisdiction over intrastate service, limiting its authority to interstate service.

[55] *Southern Railway Co. v. North Carolina et al.*, 376 U.S. 93 (1964).

[56] 210 F. Supp. 675.

[57] *Chicago, Milwaukee, St. Paul & Pacific Railroad Co. v. Illinois et al.*, 355 U.S. 300 (1958).

[58] 324 ICC 705 (1965), 324 ICC 418 (1965).

[59] Robert L. Bard, "The Challenge of Rail Passenger Service: Free Enterprise, Regulation, and Subsidy," *Univ. of Chicago Law Review*, vol. 34, 1966-1967, pp. 301-340.

[60] Even the trustees were probably not surprised by this decision. They were attempting to rid the railroad of its passenger obligations in the hopes of becoming more attractive for purchase by a merged Pennsylvania and New York Central Railroad.

[61] P.L. 91-518, Section 402.

[62] P.L. 93-146, November 3, 1973, 87 Stat. 548.

[63] ICC Annual Report, FY 1972. Several states sued to suspend this rule but the rule was upheld, 361 F. Supp. 208.

[64] U.S. DOT, *Availability and Use of Abandoned Railroad Rights-Of-Way*, June 1977.

[65] See *Chicago and North Western Transp. Co. v. United States*, 582 F.2d 1043, 1049 (7th Cir. 1978).

[66] See Elizabeth Burch Michel, "Casenote: Chicago and North Western Transportation Co. v. United States," *Transportation Law Journal*, v. 13, 1984, p. 245.

[67] Michael L. Stokes, "Adverse Abandonment: Toward Allowing the States to Condemn or Dispose of Unneeded Railroad Land," *Transportation Law Journal*, v. 31, Fall 2003, p. 69.

[68] See *Preseault v. ICC*, 494 U.S. 1 (1989).

[69] 4 ICC 2d 761 (1988).

[70] 911 F.2d 743 (D.C. Cir. 1990).

[71] The Independent Safety Board Act Amendments of 1990 (P.L. 101-641).

[72] 503 U.S. 407 (1992).

[73] "The Guilford Dilemma," *Maine Times*, March 15, 2001, p.4.

[74] *Commuter Rail: Information and Guidance Could Help Facilitate Commuter and Freight Rail Access Negotiations*, January 2004, GAO-04-240, p. 32.

[75] 1980 Annual Report of the ICC, p. 39 and *Abandonment of Railroad Lines—Use of Opportunity Costs*, 360 ICC 571, 1979.

[76] Robert E. Gallamore, "Perspectives and Prospects for American Railroad Infrastructure," *Infrastructure*, Summer1998, p. 36.

[77] *Pennsylvania Railroad v. Puritan Coal Mining Co.*, 237 U.S. 121 (1915).

[78] *Pennsylvania Railroad. v. Puritan Coal Mining Co.*, 237 U.S. 133-34 (1915).

[79] 8 ICC 2d 835 (1991).

[80] For a recent example, see Massachusetts Dept. of Transportation—Acquisition Exemption—Certain Assets of CSX Transportation, STB Docket No. FD35312, May 3, 2010. CSX railroad is selling multiple segments of its track in and around Boston to commuter operators while retaining a freight easement. In the *State of Maine* decision, the ICC cited the city of Austin's purchase of a rail line as an example where the city assumed a common carrier obligation (even though it did not intend to operate the line itself) because it acquired full ownership of the line.

[81] Kevin M. Sheys, "Strategies to Facilitate Acquisition and Use of Railroad Right of Way by Transit Providers," *Legal Research Digest, Transit Cooperative Research Program*, no. 1, September 1994.

[82] 41 Stat. 476, 477.

[83] ICC Finance Docket No. 31951 (1991).

[84] STB Finance Docket No. 33557 (1998).

[85] The potential legality of this provision from the perspective of passenger interests is discussed in Charles A. Spitulnik and Jamie Palter Rennert, "Use of Freight Rail Lines for Commuter Operations: Public Interest, Private Property," *Transportation Law Journal,* v. 26, 1999, pp. 319-339.

[86] Compare 49 U.S.C. 10501 and 49 U.S.C. 10907 before ICCTA with 49 U.S.C. 10501 after ICCTA.

[87] H.Rept. 104-311, 104th Congress, November 6, 1995, p. 95.

[88] Fritz R. Kahn, "Condemnation—An Alternative Means for Railroad Line Acquisitions," *Transportation Journal,* Fall 1993, v. 33, issue 1, p. 15.

[89] *Wisconsin Central Ltd. v. The City of Marshfield,* 160 F. Supp. 2d 1009 (2000).

[90] City of Lincoln—Petition for Declaratory Order, STB Finance Docket No. 34425, 2004 STB Lexis 508 (2004).

[91] *Soo Line Railroad Co. v. City of St. Paul,* 2010 U.S. Dist. LEXIS 59971 (2010).

[92] *Union Pacific Railroad Co. v. Chicago Transit Authority,* 647 F.3d 675 (2011).

[93] *Commuter Rail: Information and Guidance Could Help Facilitate Commuter and Freight Rail Access Negotiations,* January 2004, GAO-04-240, pp. 14-17.

[94] Jeremy Grant, "Ageing U.S. Rail Networks Stuck in a One-Track World," *Financial Times,* September 13, 2004.

[95] Testimony of Thomas F. Jansen, Vice President UPS, STB hearing, *Rail Capacity and Infrastructure Requirements,* Ex Parte No. 671, April 11, 2007.

[96] See for instance, H.R. 1617, 108th Congress.

[97] This problem is not unique to railroads. Truckers identify urban highway interchanges during rush hours as their most persistent bottlenecks.

[98] Federal Highway Administration, Office of Freight Management and Operations, *Freight Systems: From System Construction to System Optimization,* Working Paper, 2001.

In: Railroads in the United States   ISBN: 978-1-62257-727-9
Editors: Ch. E. Russel and C. M. Wood © 2013 Nova Science Publishers, Inc.

Chapter 3

INTERCITY PASSENGER AND FREIGHT RAIL: BETTER DATA AND COMMUNICATION OF UNCERTAINTIES CAN HELP DECISION MAKERS UNDERSTAND BENEFITS AND TRADE-OFFS OF PROGRAMS AND POLICIES[*]

United States Government Accountability Office

WHY GAO DID THIS STUDY

Concerns about the weak economy, congestion in the transportation system, and the potentially harmful effects of air emissions generated by the transportation sector have raised awareness of the potential benefits and costs of intercity passenger and freight rail relative to other transportation modes such as highways. GAO was asked to review (1) the extent to which transportation policy tools that provide incentives to shift passenger and freight traffic to rail may generate emissions, congestion, and economic development benefits and (2) how project benefits and costs are assessed for investment in intercity passenger and freight rail and how the strengths and limitations of these assessments impact federal decision making. GAO

---

[*] This is an edited, reformatted and augmented version of the Highlights of GAO-11-290, a report to congressional committees, dated February 2011.

reviewed studies; interviewed federal, state, local, and other stakeholders regarding methods to assess benefit and cost information; assessed information on project benefits and costs included in rail grant applications; and conducted case studies of selected policies and programs in the United Kingdom and Germany to learn more about their policies designed to provide incentives to shift traffic to rail.

WHAT GAO RECOMMENDS

GAO recommends DOT conduct a data needs assessment to improve the effectiveness of modeling and analysis for rail and provide consistent requirements for assessing rail project benefits and costs. DOT, Amtrak and EPA provided technical comments, and DOT agreed to consider the recommendations.

WHAT GAO FOUND

Although implementing policies designed to shift traffic to rail from other modes may generate benefits, and selected European countries' experiences suggest that some benefits can be achieved through these types of policies; many factors will affect whether traffic shifts. The extent to which rail can generate sufficient demand to draw traffic from other modes to achieve the desired level of net benefits will depend on numerous factors. Some passenger or freight traffic may not be substitutable or practical to move by a different mode. For example, certain freight shipments may be time-sensitive and thus cannot go by rail. Another key factor will be the extent to which sufficient capacity exists or is being planned to accommodate shifts in traffic from other modes. How transport markets respond to a given policy—such as one that changes the relative price of road transport—will also affect the level of benefits generated by that policy. Experiences in selected countries suggest that varying amounts of mode shift and some benefits were attained where decision makers implemented policies to move traffic from other modes to rail. For example, a road freight pricing policy in Germany resulted in environmental and efficiency improvements, and freight rail grants in the United Kingdom led to congestion relief at the country's largest port. Pursuing policies to encourage traffic to shift to rail is one potential way to generate benefits, and other policies may be implemented to generate specific benefits at a potentially lower cost.

Information on the benefits and costs of intercity passenger and freight rail is assessed to varying degrees by those seeking federal funding for investment in rail projects; however, data limitations and other factors reduce the usefulness of such assessments for federal decision makers. Applicants to two discretionary federal grant programs—the Transportation Investment Generating Economic Recovery program and the High-Speed Intercity Passenger Rail program—provided assessments of potential project benefits and costs that were generally not comprehensive. For instance, applications varied widely in the extent to which they quantified and monetized some categories of benefits. In addition, GAO's assessment of selected applications found that most applicants did not provide key information recommended in federal guidance for such assessments, including information related to uncertainty in projections, data limitations, or the assumptions underlying their models. Applicants, industry experts, and Department of Transportation (DOT) officials GAO spoke with reported that many challenges impacted their ability to produce useful assessments of project benefits and costs, including: short time frames in which to prepare the assessments, limited resources and expertise for performing assessments, poor data quality, lack of access to data, and lack of standard values for monetizing some benefits. As a result, while information on project benefits and costs was considered as one of many factors in the decision-making process, according to DOT officials, the varying quality and focus of assessments resulted in additional work, and the information provided was of limited usefulness to DOT decision makers.

ABBREVIATIONS

AAR	Association of American Railroads
BTS	Bureau of Transportation Statistics
DOT	Department of Transportation
EPA	Environmental Protection Agency
FAA	Federal Aviation Administration
FAF	Freight Analysis Framework
FHWA	Federal Highway Administration
FRA	Federal Railroad Administration
HGV	Heavy Goods Vehicle

HSIPR	High-Speed Intercity Passenger Rail Program
ITIC	Intermodal Transportation and Inventory Cost Model
NHTSA	National Highway Traffic Safety Administration
OMB	Office of Management and Budget
PRIIA	Passenger Rail Investment and Improvement Act of 2008
Recovery Act	American Recovery and Reinvestment Act of 2009
RRIF	Railroad Rehabilitation and Improvement Financing
SAFETEA-LU	Safe, Accountable, Flexible, Efficient Transportation Equity Act: A Legacy for Users
TIFIA	Transportation Infrastructure Finance and Innovation Act
TIGER	Transportation Investment Generating Economic Recovery
VMT	vehicle miles traveled

February 24, 2011

The Honorable John D. Rockefeller IV
Chairman
The Honorable Kay Bailey Hutchison
Ranking Member
Committee on Commerce, Science, and Transportation
United States Senate

The Honorable Frank R. Lautenberg
Chairman
The Honorable John Thune
Ranking Member
Subcommittee on Surface Transportation and Merchant Marine Infrastructure, Safety and Security
Committee on Commerce, Science, and Transportation
United States Senate

Concerns about the weak economy, congestion in the transportation system, and the potentially harmful effects of greenhouse gases and airborne pollutants from transportation have raised awareness of the potential benefits and costs of intercity passenger and freight rail relative to other transportation modes. The U.S. economy and its competitive position in the global economy depend in part on the nation's transportation networks working efficiently. In addition, factors such as cost and time can impact passengers' and shippers' demand for a particular transportation mode. Congestion delays that significantly constrain both passenger and freight mobility can result in increased economic costs to passengers, shippers and also to the nation. According to the Texas Transportation Institute, in 2009 the yearly peak-period delay per auto commuter was 34 hours, with a total cost of $115 billion.[1] Continued development and efficient management of the nation's transportation system is essential to accommodate the anticipated future growth of the nation's passenger and freight mobility demands. For example, the Department of Transportation (DOT) forecasts that between 2010 and 2035 the freight transportation system will experience a 22 percent increase in total freight tonnage moved in the United States, from 12.5 billion to 15.3 billion tons.[2] In addition, the transportation industry continues to be one of the biggest energy users and contributors to greenhouse gas emissions. According to the Environmental Protection Agency (EPA), for 2008 the transportation sector accounts for 27 percent of the nation's greenhouse gas emissions.[3] Because shifting intercity passenger and freight traffic to rail from other more energy-intensive modes is seen as a potential option to address some of these concerns, there is a growing interest in investing in and enhancing rail capacity and implementing policies that will encourage more traffic by rail.[4]

The Passenger Rail Investment and Improvement Act (PRIIA), enacted in October 2008,[5] authorized over $3.7 billion for three different federal programs for high-speed rail,[6] intercity passenger rail congestion,[7] and intercity passenger rail service corridor capital grants.[8] The American Recovery and Reinvestment Act of 2009 (Recovery Act), enacted in February 2009, appropriated $8 billion for the three PRIIA-established intercity passenger rail programs. In addition, the Recovery Act authorized new discretionary grants under the Transportation Investment Generating Economic Recovery (TIGER) program.[9]

PRIIA and the Recovery Act created new responsibilities for Federal Railroad Administration (FRA) to plan, award, and oversee the use of new federal funds for intercity passenger rail. In response, FRA launched the High-Speed Intercity Passenger Rail (HSIPR) program in June 2009 by issuing a funding announcement and interim guidance, that outlined the requirements and procedures for obtaining federal funds.[10] Moreover, in 2010 DOT awarded over $2 billion in TIGER and $10 billion in HSIPR grants. Both programs required applications to include information on the costs and benefits of proposed projects, including information on such benefits as reducing environmental impacts and congestion and encouraging economic development.

One of the many considerations that can help inform transportation decision making is determining which investment or set of policies will yield the greatest net benefit (that is, benefits minus costs). While there is some debate around the extent to which investment in rail or policies that encourage shifting traffic to rail from other modes can help address problems, such as congestion and greenhouse gas emissions, there are a variety of analytical approaches, such as benefit-cost analysis and others, that may be employed to help evaluate proposed transportation investments. Tools such as these can provide decision makers with information on the benefits and costs of alternative investments and policy choices needed to make informed decisions. Given your interest in the potential net benefits of intercity passenger and freight rail policies and programs, we examined (1) the extent to which transportation policy tools that provide incentives to shift passenger and freight traffic to rail may generate emissions, congestion, and economic development benefits and (2) how project benefits and costs are assessed for investment in intercity passenger and freight rail and how the strengths and limitations of these assessments impact federal decision making.

To address our objectives, we reviewed our prior work on rail and transportation investment decision making and documentation from an array of sources, as well as interviewing officials and various stakeholders regarding methods to assess the benefits and costs of transportation investments. Our interviews included discussions with officials from DOT, EPA, and the National Railroad Passenger Corporation (Amtrak); representatives from transportation coalitions and associations, metropolitan planning organizations, and state DOTs; and other transportation stakeholders. We also reviewed and assessed information on potential project benefits and costs included in 40 rail-related applications submitted to the HSIPR and TIGER grant programs—20 from each program. We selected a random sample of applications that was weighted to ensure approximately proportional representation of the range of applications submitted to each program. Two GAO analysts independently reviewed each selected application based on Office of Management and Budget (OMB) guidelines on benefit-cost analysis,[11] with input from GAO economists and methodologists. We conducted an extensive literature search to identify studies analyzing potential mode shift and the impact of mode shift on selected benefits for intercity passenger or freight rail projects and policies. We used the studies and information we reviewed to inform our work and relied on multiple sources of additional information, including testimonial evidence, interviews, and case studies. We conducted case studies of selected policies and programs designed to provide incentives to shift passenger and freight traffic from other modes to rail in the United Kingdom and Germany to learn more about their experiences with efforts to shift traffic to rail in order to generate benefits. These two countries were chosen based on a number of criteria, including their experience in implementing such policies. While European intercity passenger and freight rail systems are very different in size, structure, and scope than the U.S. rail system, the experiences of countries such as the United Kingdom and Germany provide illustrative examples of other countries' experiences with policy tools that provide incentives to shift traffic to rail.[12] Finally, we conducted our own computer simulation of transportation scenarios on mode choice for freight shipments. See appendix IV for a discussion of the simulation and appendix I for a detailed discussion of our scope and methodology.

We conducted this performance audit from December 2009 to February 2011, in accordance with generally accepted government auditing standards. Those standards require that we plan and perform the audit to obtain sufficient, appropriate evidence to provide a reasonable basis for our findings and conclusions based on our audit objectives. We believe the evidence obtained provides a reasonable basis for our findings and conclusions based on our audit objectives.

BACKGROUND

Passenger and freight rail are part of a complex national transportation system for transporting people and goods. Currently, there are seven Class I railroads and over 500 short line and regional railroads operating in the United States.[13] These railroads operate the nation's freight rail system and own the majority of rail infrastructure in the United States. Railroads are the primary mode of transportation for many products, especially for such bulk commodities as coal and grain. In addition, railroads are carrying increasing levels of intermodal freight (e.g., containers and trailers), which travel on multiple modes and typically require faster delivery than bulk commodities. According to the Association of American Railroads (AAR), based on ton-miles, freight railroads carried about 43 percent of domestic intercity freight volume in 2009. In addition, according to DOT, the amount of freight rail is expected to continue to grow with a projected increase of nearly 22 percent by 2035. Intercity passenger rail service is primarily provided by Amtrak. Amtrak operates a 21,000-mile network, which provides service to 46 states and Washington, D.C., primarily over tracks owned by freight railroads. Federal law requires that freight railroads give Amtrak trains preference over freight transportation and, in general, charge Amtrak the incremental cost—rather than an apportioned cost—associated with the use of their tracks.[14] Amtrak also owns about 650 route miles of track, primarily on the Northeast Corridor, which runs between Boston, Massachusetts, and Washington, D.C.

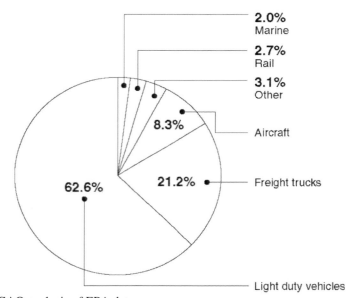

Source: GAO analysis of EPA data.

Note: "Light duty vehicles" includes passenger cars and light duty trucks. "Freight trucks" includes heavy and medium trucks. "Marine" includes ships and boats. For Marine, the source indicates that emission estimates reflect data collection problems. "Other" includes motorcycles, lubricants, buses, and pipelines.

Figure 1. 2008 Estimates of U.S. Greenhouse Gas Emissions by Transportation Mode.

Transportation may impose a variety of "external" costs that can result in impacts such as health and environmental damage caused by pollution.[15] For example, in choosing to drive to work, a commuter may not take into account the car emissions' contribution to local pollution, which may damage property or the health of others. Following are some negative effects of transportation:

- *Greenhouse gas emissions, nitrogen oxide (NO_X) and fine particulate matter, and other pollutants:* Based on estimated data from the EPA, from 1990 through 2008, transportation greenhouse gas emissions increased 22 percent. Carbon dioxide (CO_2) is the primary greenhouse gas associated with the combustion of diesel (and other fossil fuels) and accounted for over 95.5 percent of the transportation sector's greenhouse gas emissions.[16] Based on 2008 data from the EPA, cars, light trucks, and freight trucks together contributed over 80 percent of the transportation sector greenhouse gas emissions (see figure 1).[17]
  In addition, NOX and fine particulate matter with a diameter of 2.5 microns or less (PM2.5) contribute to air pollution. Both of these pollutants are emitted through high temperature combustion and activities such as burning fossil fuels. For 2002, based on our analysis of EPA data, it was estimated that trucks emitted 3.02 tons of NOX and .12 tons of PM2.5 per million ton-miles.18

- *Congestion:* While congestion is geographically concentrated in metropolitan areas, international trade gateways, and on some intercity trade routes, congestion is a serious problem, contributing to longer and more unpredictable transit times and resulting in increased transportation costs. The Texas Transportation Institute estimates that for 439 domestic urban areas, congestion costs in 2009 alone were $115 billion and accounted for a total of 3.9 billion gallons of gasoline consumption. For freight, congestion delays that significantly constrain freight mobility could result in increased economic costs for the nation. The Federal Highway Administration (FHWA) has calculated that delays caused by highway bottlenecks cost the trucking industry alone more than $8 billion a year. Similarly, we have previously reported on the significant level of congestion that exists, and is expected to grow, at airports in large urban areas throughout the country. The Federal Aviation Administration (FAA) predicts that, by 2025, the number of airline passengers will increase 57 percent—from about 700 million to about 1.1 billion per year—and the number of daily flights will increase from about 80,000 to more than 95,000. Today's air transportation system will be strained to meet this growth in air traffic.[19]

- *Accidents:* Each year, there are tens of thousands of truck and vehicle accidents that result in injury or fatality. Based on National Highway

Traffic Safety Administration (NHTSA) data, there were 33,808 fatal motor vehicle crashes in the United States in 2009. This resulted in a national motor vehicle death rate of 1.13 deaths per 100 million vehicle miles traveled (VMT). For freight, preliminary data from DOT for 2009 shows the rate of fatalities involving large trucks and buses was 0.121 per 100 million VMT. A portion of motor vehicle crash costs are not covered by private insurance. According to a 2000 NHTSA report, approximately $21 billion, or 9 percent of all costs are borne by public sources. Similarly, we estimated truck external accident costs of $8,000 per million ton-miles that are not passed on to consumers.[20]

Investment and Policy Tools to Attain Benefits through Rail

While there are multiple approaches to address externalities in transportation, policies that provide incentives to shift traffic to rail can be appealing because they offer an option to address multiple externalities simultaneously by changing behavior to favor rail over other modes. For example, market-based policies that change the relative prices of the modes are likely going to be the most cost-effective. Policies such as increasing fuel taxes, imposing new fees such as a vehicle mile travel fee or a congestion charge, investing in increased capacity in one mode, or subsidizing travel in one mode can provide incentives to users to switch travel from one mode to another, and can achieve both a reduction in greenhouse gas emissions and alleviate congestion.[21] Some stakeholders also believe that investing in rail may help to stimulate economic development. In order to obtain similar benefits without the goal of shifting traffic to rail, it might be necessary to introduce a suite of policies, each more directly targeted at a specific externality.[22] For example, a congestion pricing policy may reduce traffic during peak travel times, but if it shifts traffic to nonpeak times, it may have a limited impact on overall emissions. Conversely, providing incentives to purchase more fuel efficient truck engines may do nothing to improve congestion or economic development.

With respect to direct investment, the federal government typically has not provided extensive funding for freight rail or for intercity passenger rail outside of the Northeast Corridor between Boston, Massachusetts and Washington, D.C. In addition, according to Amtrak officials, funding has not been predictable, consistent, or sustained. However, recent legislation has increased the federal role and funding available for investment in intercity passenger and freight rail infrastructure. In 2008, PRIIA authorized the HSIPR program.[23] The program is administered through DOT's FRA, which has responsibility for planning, awarding, and overseeing the use of federal funds for the development of high-speed and intercity passenger rail.[24] As of 2010, over $10 billion had been awarded through the HSIPR program to fund high-speed rail projects.[25] Moreover, through the Recovery Act, Congress authorized the TIGER Discretionary Grant Program for investment in a variety of transportation areas, including freight and passenger rail.[26] In 2010, DOT awarded over $2 billion in TIGER funding. The TIGER program was designed to preserve and create jobs and to promote economic recovery and investment in transportation infrastructure that will provide long-term economic benefits and assist those most affected by the current economic downturn. The TIGER grants are multimodal, and criteria were developed for a framework to assess projects across various modes. For more information on the HSIPR and TIGER programs, see appendix III.[27]

Assessment of Benefits and Costs in Decision Making

Decision makers may consider a number of factors in deciding between various alternative investments or policies. These factors may include the objective or goal of the proposed actions—for example, preserving and creating jobs or promoting economic recovery or reducing an environmental externality. Other factors, such as the benefits and costs of alternatives, are also important to consider in decision making. Some benefits are associated with reducing an externality and are part of the assessment of whether policy alternatives for addressing the externality can be justified on economic principles.[28] Costs should also be accounted for when considering various investment or policy alternatives. For example, there are direct costs, such as construction, maintenance, and operations, and less obvious types of costs, such as delays and pollution generated during construction.

There are tools that can be employed in evaluating proposed transportation alternatives, including benefit-cost analysis[29] and economic impact analysis. Benefit-cost analysis is designed to identify the alternative with the greatest net benefit by comparing the monetary value of benefits and costs of each alternative with a baseline. Benefit-cost analysis provides for a comparison of alternatives based on economic efficiency, that is, which investment or policy would provide the greatest net benefit (i.e., greater benefits than costs). As we have previously reported, while benefit-cost analysis may not be the most important decision-making factor—but rather, one of many tools that decision makers may use to organize, evaluate, and determine trade-offs of various alternatives—the increased use of systematic analytical tools such as benefit-cost analysis can provide important additional information that can lead to better informed transportation decision making.[30] Economic impact analysis is a tool for assessing how the benefits and costs of transportation alternatives would be distributed throughout the economy and for identifying groups in society (for example, by region, income, or race) that are likely to gain from, or bear the costs of, a policy.

The use of benefit-cost analysis information is not consistent across modes or types of programs that provide funding to transportation projects. Competitive programs such as TIGER and HSIPR and loan guarantee programs such as TIFIA and RRIF require information on benefits and costs.[31] Formula programs (such as the Federal-Aid Highway Program)[32] do not necessarily require benefit-cost information. Federal guidance exists for conducting benefit-cost analyses, including OMB Circular No. A-94, OMB Circular No. A-4, and Executive Order No. 12893. The directive and related OMB guidance outline a number of key elements that should be included in the assessment of benefits and costs in decision making, as described in table 1.

Specifically Executive Order No. 12893 and OMB Circulars Nos. A-94 and A-4 indicate that benefit and cost information shall be used in decision making, and the level of uncertainty in estimates of benefits and costs shall be disclosed.[33] Other aspects of the benefit-cost analysis should be completed to the extent possible. For example, while the guidance suggests that impacts should be quantified and monetized, to the extent that this is not possible, qualitative assessments should be provided for those impacts that are not readily quantifiable. As we have previously reported in our work on transit investments, qualitative information can help ensure that project impacts that cannot be easily quantified are considered in decision making.[34]

Both the HSIPR and TIGER grant programs required applicants to provide information on proposed project benefits and costs. The type of information required, however, differed between the two programs and, for the TIGER program, depended on the level of federal funding sought, as described in table 2. In addition, while requirements for assessment of project benefits and costs were more specific for TIGER than for the HSIPR program, officials for both programs considered whether project benefits were likely to exceed project costs as part of their respective application assessment processes.

Table 1. Key Elements for Benefit-Cost Analysis from Presidential Exec. Order No. 12893 and OMB Circulars Nos. A-94 and A-4

Comparison to base case and alternatives	Establish a base case for comparison.
	Identify alternative projects—benefits and costs should be defined in comparison with a clearly stated alternative.
Analysis of benefits and costs	Define a time frame for analysis.
	Quantify and monetize impacts as benefits and costs to the maximum extent possible, but consider qualitative measures reflecting values that are not readily quantified.
	Measure and discount benefits and costs over the full life cycle of the project and identify the year in which dollars are presented.
Transparency of information and treatment of uncertainty	Clearly state all assumptions underlying the analysis of benefits and costs.
	Assess the sensitivity of the analysis to changes in assumptions and forecasted inputs and recognize uncertainty through appropriate quantitative and qualitative assessments.

Sources: GAO analysis of Presidential Exec. Order No. 12893 and OMB Circulars Nos. A-94 and A-4.

SHIFTING TRAFFIC TO RAIL FROM OTHER MODES MAY GENERATE BENEFITS, BUT MANY FACTORS WILL AFFECT WHETHER TRAFFIC SHIFTS, AND POLICIES ABROAD HAVE PRODUCED MIXED RESULTS

Determining the Extent of Benefits that can be Achieved through Rail Is Complicated by Numerous Factors

In order to generate benefits—such as a decrease in the harmful effects of transportation-related pollution—through mode shift, a policy first has to attract sufficient rail ridership or rail freight demand from other modes that have higher harmful emissions. In practice, the extent to which rail can generate sufficient demand to draw traffic from other modes and generate net benefits will depend on numerous factors.[35] In addition to mode shift, policies that produce price changes can prompt other economic responses in the short run, such as the use of lighter-weight materials or a shift toward more fuel-efficient vehicles; over the longer term, there is greater potential for responses that will shape the overall distribution and use of freight and passenger transportation services.[36]

Table 2. Federal Discretionary Transportation Grant Program Requirements for Assessments of Project Benefits and Costs

Grant program	Size of grant sought	Program requirements for assessment of benefits and costs	Benefit-cost guidance referred to in the Federal Register
TIGER	Less than $20 million	Information on project benefits and costs not required.	Exec. Order No.12893 and OMB Circular Nos. A-94 and A-4
	Between $20 million and $100 million	Required to include estimates of the projects' expected benefits in five long-term outcome categories: (1) state of good repair, (2) economic competitiveness, (3) livability, (4) sustainability, and (5) safety.[a]	
	More than $100 million	Required to provide a "well developed" analysis of expected benefits and costs, including calculation of net benefits and a description of input data and methodological standards used for the analysis.	
HSIPR	Any amount	Required to provide information on public return on investment in three categories: (1) transportation benefits, (2) economic recovery benefits, and (3) public benefits, which include energy independence and efficiency, environmental quality, and livable communities. Applications to HSIPR were divided into four groups, each of which required assessments of public return on investment in these categories. However, importance of benefit categories varied across these groups (see app. III).	Exec. Order No.12893

Source: GAO analysis of TIGER and HSIPR *Federal Register* notices.

Note: For TIGER II—the second round of TIGER funding that DOT awarded in October 2010—DOT required benefit-cost analyses from all applicants, regardless of the amount of funding requested.

[a] According to DOT, projects that contribute to a state of good repair by improving the condition of existing facilities and transportation systems; projects that meet economic competitiveness criteria contribute to the economic competitiveness of the United States over the medium-term and long-term; projects that meet livability criteria improve the quality of living and working environments and experience for people in communities across the United States; projects that meet sustainability criteria improve energy efficiency, reduce dependence on oil, reduce greenhouse gas emissions, and benefit the environment; and projects that meet safety criteria improve the safety of U.S. transportation facilities and systems.

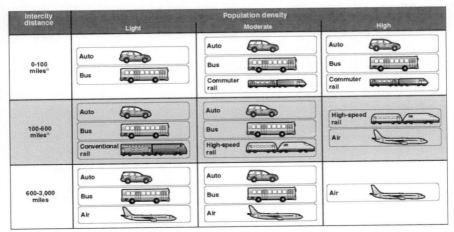

Source: GAO analysis of DOT information.
[a] In certain corridors in high-density areas, conventional rail also competes with other modes (e.g., New York to Philadelphia).

Figure 2. Competition among Passenger Transportation Modes.

For intercity passenger rail, factors such as high levels of population density, expected population growth along a corridor, and strong business and cultural ties between cities can lead to a higher demand for intercity passenger travel. In order for rail to be competitive with other transportation modes, it needs to be time- and price-competitive and have favorable service characteristics related to frequency, reliability, and safety. Further, high-speed rail has more potential to attract riders in corridors experiencing heavy intercity travel on existing modes of transportation—particularly where air transportation has high traffic levels and a large share of the market over relatively short distances—and where there is, or is projected to be, growth in congestion and constraints on the capacity of existing systems. For example, rail traffic in the densely populated Northeast Corridor is highly competitive with other modes, and Amtrak now has a 65 percent share of the air-rail market between Washington, D.C. and New York and a 52 percent share between New York and Boston.[37] The potential for network effects are also an important factor in the level of traffic that may shift to rail, as more riders are attracted when the line is located where it can carry traffic to a wide number of destinations or connect to other modes. For example, local transit systems can serve as feeders to the success of intercity passenger rail operations.[38] Passenger modes can also work as complements, if, for example, passenger rail service delivers passengers to airports. DOT has indicated where passenger rail generally competes with other modes. For example, for intercity distances of 100-600 miles, in corridors with moderate population densities, high-speed rail competes with auto and bus and at high population densities competes with air, as shown in figure 2.[39]

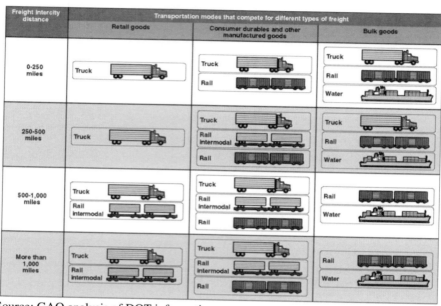

Source: GAO analysis of DOT information.

Figure 3. Competition among Freight Transportation Modes.

In freight markets, one mode may have a distinct comparative advantage over another for certain types of shipments, thereby limiting the potential for traffic to shift to rail. For example, carriage of bulk commodities (e.g., coal) relies almost entirely on rail and waterways, while carriage of high-value and very time-sensitive commodities is dominated by truck and aviation. Conversely, modes often work as complements to complete a shipment. Intermodal freight is designed to move on multiple modes, using a container that can be moved from a truck to a train to a ship without handling any of the freight itself when changing modes. In other cases, the modes may be substitutable for certain types of trips and will compete directly for shipments or for segments of shipments based on price and performance. For example, some long-haul trucking and rail shipments may be substitutable. DOT has produced some basic parameters that influence competition across the modes for freight, as shown in figure 3.

The extent to which mode-shifting is possible in the United States is difficult to estimate and will largely be determined by the types of parameters discussed above, such as whether shipping is feasible by another mode (e.g., rail lines may not be available for some routes), or practical (e.g., sending heavy coal shipments long distance by truck or time-sensitive shipments by rail may not be practical), and by the relative prices and other service characteristics of shipping by different modes.

To further explore the potential for mode shift, we used a computer model developed by DOT[40] to simulate the short-term change in VMT resulting from a 50-cent increase in per-mile truck rates. We simulated two scenarios: one using the model's default assumptions and one in which the assumptions pertaining to truck speed, reliability, and loss and damage were adjusted to make truck relatively more costly than rail.[41] Under both scenarios, the 50-cent increase in truck rates (an increase of roughly 30 percent) resulted in less than a 1 percent decrease in truck VMT. Although both the default scenario and the alternative scenario produced similar estimates, these simulations are only suggestive, rather than definitive, of the impact that an increase in per-mile truck rates might have on VMT reduction. While the results of our simulation suggest that a 50-cent increase in per-mile truck rates would have a limited impact on diversion of freight from truck to rail, data limitations prevent us from making precise predictions with a high level of confidence. See appendix IV for a more detailed description of our modeling efforts, data quality issues, and a full list of assumptions in the model.

In both the United States and in other countries we visited—where freight and passenger traffic generally share the same rail infrastructure— the potential benefits of a policy designed to shift freight traffic to rail are also affected by the amount of capacity available or planned on the rail network to accommodate a shift in traffic, as well as the capacity available or planned on competing transportation modes. For example, freight rail officials we met with in the United States indicated that in heavily congested corridors, such as in the Northeast, there is limited capacity available to accommodate both planned freight rail projects and proposed intercity passenger rail traffic, because the rail line is already congested. Plans for new dedicated high-speed rail lines would eliminate some of these capacity sharing issues and could potentially create the capacity needed to accommodate both freight and improved or expanded passenger service but must be weighed against the costs associated with constructing and maintaining new equipment and infrastructure, as well as acquiring rights of way for the track.[42] Furthermore, significant investment and improvements to operations for highway infrastructure or airport infrastructure could offset the impact of policies designed to shift passenger or freight traffic to rail. For example, the FAA is currently pursuing modernization of the air transportation system to create additional capacity and efficiencies. If, as a result, flights become more efficient and travel times decrease, then travelers originally expected to shift to rail as a result of the implemented policy may not do so. In contrast, the existence of other policies in place concurrently may also be a contributing factor to improvements in environmental or congestion benefits, as separate policies may work together and lead to greater cumulative benefits. In either case, it can be difficult to distinguish the impact of a given policy due to these other factors.

Following are descriptions of how shifting traffic to rail can address externalities and produce benefits, as well as some of the factors that affect the extent to which those benefits may materialize:

Reduced greenhouse gas emissions and increased fuel efficiency: Rail emits fewer air emissions and is generally more fuel efficient than trucks. For example, a report by the American Association of State Highway and Transportation Officials (AASHTO) cites that the American Society of Mechanical Engineers estimates 2.5 million fewer tons of carbon dioxide would be emitted into the air annually if 10 percent of intercity freight now moving by highway were shifted to rail, if such traffic has the potential to shift.[43] A recent study conducted by FRA comparing the fuel efficiency of rail to freight trucks calculated that rail had fuel efficiencies ranging from 156 to 512 ton-miles per gallon, while trucks had fuel efficiencies ranging from 68 to 133 ton-miles per gallon.[44] According to Amtrak officials, their intercity passenger rail service has also been shown to be more energy efficient than air or passenger vehicle traffic.[45] In addition, passenger and freight rail can be electrified to eliminate even current emissions generated by rail transport, as alternative power (e.g., hydro or nuclear) may be used to generate electric propulsion. For example, many of the routes in the United Kingdom are electrified, and efforts are under way to continue to electrify additional segments of the rail network in order to reduce emissions. While rail generally provides favorable emissions attributes and fuel efficiency in comparison with highway and air travel, there are many factors that could affect the extent to which environmental benefits are achieved. These factors may include the type of train equipment, the mix of commodities being transported, the length of the rail route versus the truck route for a given shipment, traffic volume, and capacity. In addition, if the current transportation system is not designed to facilitate rail transport, it may be necessary to invest in additional capital infrastructure or build new rail yards closer to urban areas, which could have additional environmental costs and may diminish the extent of potential net benefits. Furthermore, how transport system users respond to a given policy will also impact the extent to which the policy generates any benefits. For example, a policy that changes the price of road transport by tolling could result in a freight hauler responding by changing the load factor of existing road shipments by consolidating shipments or increasing return loads to decrease the number of empty return trips. A similar policy could also lead to reduced transport volumes due to reduced demand for the product being shipped. According to DOT officials, correctly pricing usage of the transportation system is an ongoing challenge, as incorrect pricing can lead to inefficiencies and misallocation of resources beyond what market conditions would otherwise allow. Other policies aside from mode shift can more directly target environmental externalities. More targeted policies—such as increasing fuel taxes or implementing a carbon pricing scheme—may encourage drivers to purchase more fuel-efficient vehicles or make fewer vehicle trips, without shifting significant traffic to rail.

Congestion: Where passenger or freight rail service provides a less costly alternative to other modes—through more timely or reliable transport—individuals and shippers can shift out of more congested modes and onto rail, thus alleviating congestion. For certain goods, a train can generally carry the freight of 280 or more trucks, relieving congestion by removing freight trucks from the highways.[46] Similarly, an intercity passenger train can carry many times more people than the typical passenger vehicle.[47] Consequently, if fewer vehicle miles are traveled, then there is less wear and tear on the highways and less cost to the public for related repairs and maintenance. However, congestion relief will vary based on specific locations, times of day, types of trips being diverted to another mode, and the conditions of the corridors and areas where trips are being diverted. For freight, long-haul shipments might have the most potential to shift to rail, but diversion of these trips to rail, while removing trucks from certain stretches of highway, may do little to address problems at the most congested bottlenecks in urban areas. Similarly, Amtrak officials noted that aviation can provide travelers' alternative options for travel in high-density corridors which may help relieve congestion at capacity-constrained airports. If high-speed rail can divert travelers from making an intercity trip through congested highway bottlenecks or airports at peak travel times, then there may be a noticeable effect on traffic. However, any trips on a congested highway corridor that are diverted to another mode of travel, such as rail, may at least partially be replaced by other trips through induced demand. For example, since congestion has been reduced on a highway, making it easier to travel, more people may respond by choosing to drive on that highway where faster travel times are available, limiting the relief in the long-run. Other policies can be implemented that are designed to more directly address congestion where it is most acute, such as congestion pricing (e.g., converting high-occupancy vehicle lanes to high-occupancy toll lanes) or other demand management strategies.

Safety: While safety has improved across all transportation modes over time, both passenger and freight rail may have a comparative advantage over other modes. Shippers and passengers who use rail in lieu of other modes may accrue measurable safety benefits because rail traffic is, for the most part, separated from other traffic. Because most rail accidents—both injuries and fatalities—involve traffic at limited locations such as grade crossings or on railroad property, safety benefits can be expected when more traffic is moved via rail. On a per-mile basis, passenger and freight rail are substantially safer than cars or trucks. For example, according to Amtrak, there were 8 passenger fatalities between 2003 and 2007. In addition, in 2007 most freight accidents occurred on highways—over 6 million—as compared with rail, which accounted for approximately 5,400 accidents. Between 2003 and 2007, freight rail averaged 0.39 fatalities per billion ton-miles, compared with 2.54 fatalities per billion ton-miles for truck.[48] There are a variety of policies and regulations that directly address safety concerns for each mode (e.g., safety standards and inspections for rail, vehicle safety features, etc.).

Economic development: The recent economic downturn has spurred interest in developing opportunities to preserve and create jobs in order to help promote economic recovery. According to DOT, investment in intercity passenger and freight rail may aid in the short-term creation of jobs and potentially in the long-term development of higher density economic activity through concentrating retail and commercial business activity near rail lines or stations. Investment in intercity passenger and freight rail may be viewed as a potential avenue to generate economic development and produce wider economic impacts.[49] Wider economic impacts associated with the investment in rail may include such things as added regional and national economic output and higher productivity and lower infrastructure costs. For example, investment in intercity high-speed passenger rail service could significantly influence the nature of regional economies beyond employment and income growth related to the investment in a rail system by spurring increases in business activity through travel efficiency gains. Moreover, the existence of new transport hubs and corridors creates the potential for economic development, as businesses may start to operate in the newly developed area in and around the rail corridor over the medium-term and the long-term. However, in some cases, these types of impacts may reflect transfers of economic activity from one region to another and thus may not be viewed as benefits from a national perspective, or these impacts may already be accounted for through users' direct benefits. As such, there is much debate about achieving these wider economic impacts and a number of challenges associated with assessing these types of impacts. While high-speed rail may have wider economic impacts, the impact varies greatly from case to case and is difficult to predict. Estimates of benefits vary, as one study has suggested that wider economic benefits would not generally exceed 10 to 20 percent of measured benefits, while an evaluation of another proposed high-speed rail line estimated these benefits to add 40 percent to direct benefits.[50] There are a variety of other policies that could be implemented to help stimulate economic development without mode shift.

In Selected European Countries, Experiences Suggest That Policies Intended to Produce Mode Shift May Lead to Varying Amounts of Mode Shift and Some Benefits

Based on experience in the United Kingdom and Germany where decision makers made a concerted effort to move traffic from other modes to rail through pricing policies, targeted grants, and infrastructure investments, these policies resulted in varying amounts of mode shift.[51] The full extent of benefits generated from these policies is ultimately uncertain, though benefits realized included environmental and efficiency improvements or localized congestion relief. Foreign rail officials told us it was difficult to determine the full extent of the benefits due to complicating factors (as described throughout the previous section). While some benefits were attained through implementation of policies designed to shift traffic to rail, these benefits were not necessarily achieved in the manner originally anticipated or at the level originally estimated. Furthermore, it is uncertain whether the benefits attained were achieved in the most efficient manner, or whether similar benefits could have been attained through other policies at a lower cost.

Road freight pricing policies: In 2005, the German government implemented a Heavy Goods Vehicle (HGV) tolling policy on motorways to generate revenue to further upgrade and maintain the transportation system and to introduce infrastructure charging based on the "user pays" principle by changing the relative price of road transport relative to rail. The HGV tolling policy was also designed to provide an incentive to shift approximately 10 percent of road freight traffic to rail and waterways in the interests of the environment and to deploy HGVs more efficiently. According to German Ministry of Transport officials, while the HGV toll policy did not result in the amount of mode shift originally anticipated, some level of environmental benefits and road freight industry efficiency improvements were realized. These benefits are attributed to a more fuel-efficient HGV fleet making fewer empty trips. For example, officials told us that, in response to the tolling policy, trucking companies purchased more lower emission vehicles, which were charged a lower per-mile rate in order to decrease their toll.[52] For the most part, German freight shipments continued to be made primarily on trucks, and trucks' mode share has not changed appreciably since instituting the policy. Findings in a study conducted for the Ministry of Transport also indicated that transport on lower emission trucks has increased significantly, totaling 49 percent of all freight operations subject to tolls in 2009. According to German transport officials, the share of freight moved by rail has only slightly increased during the last decade. However, this increase cannot be clearly attributed to a particular policy tool, such as the HGV toll.

Other countries have had similar experiences implementing pricing policies to provide incentives to shift traffic to rail. For example, the Swiss government implemented a HGV fee in 2001 on all roads to encourage freight traffic to shift from road to rail. This policy similarly resulted in improved efficiency because the trucking industry adapted its fleet and replaced some high emission vehicles with new lower emission vehicles. According to Swiss Federal Office of Transport documentation, HGV traffic through the Swiss Alps also decreased compared with what it would have been without introduction of the fee. However, to fully assess the magnitude of benefits of these types of tolling policies, these improvements would need to be weighed against the costs of implementing the policy, and this type of analysis has not been conducted.

Freight rail operations and capital support: The United Kingdom's Department for Transport uses two grant programs providing financial support for specific rail freight projects to encourage mode shift and provide congestion relief, based on the view that road freight generally does not pay its share of the significant external costs that it creates. The department's Mode Shift Revenue Support scheme provides funding for operational expenses and the Freight Facilities Grant program supplements capital projects for freight infrastructure. The British government's experience with these policies—which draw from a relatively small pool of annual funding and are intentionally designed to serve a targeted market—led to localized benefits for particular segments of the freight transport market in specific geographic locations such as congested bottlenecks near major ports. An evaluation of the Freight Facilities Grants program found that the program funding played an important role in developing or retaining rail freight flows, traditionally focused on bulk commodities.[53] According to officials we met with, the grants from the Mode Shift Revenue Support scheme encourage mode shift principally for the economically important and growing intermodal container market and have been successful in reducing congestion on specific road freight routes because the program focuses on container flows from major ports (in which rail now has a 25 percent market share). These officials noted that, out of approximately 800,000 truck journeys removed from the road as a result of the grants from the Mode Shift Revenue Support scheme, between 2009 and 2010, 450,000 trucks were removed from England's largest port—the Port of Felixstowe. Therefore, officials said the grants appear to have led to a decrease in truck traffic concentrated in specific locations for a particular segment of the freight transport industry.

Intercity passenger rail infrastructure investments: Few postimplementation studies have been conducted to empirically assess the benefits resulting from investment in high-speed intercity passenger rail. Based on our previous work, some countries that have invested in new high-speed intercity passenger rail services have experienced discernable mode shift from air to rail where rail is trip-time competitive. For example, the introduction of high-speed intercity rail lines in France and Spain led to a decrease in air travel with an increase in rail ridership, and Air France officials estimated that high-speed rail is likely to capture about 80 percent of the air-rail market when rail journey times are between 2 and 3 hours.[54] For example, with the introduction of the Madrid-Barcelona high-speed rail line in February 2008, air travel dropped an estimated 30 percent. In France, high-speed rail has captured 90 percent of the Paris-Lyon air-rail market. While discernible mode shift has been observed, the extent to which net benefits were achieved is unclear. Factors such as the proportion of traffic diverted from air or conventional rail versus newly generated traffic affect the extent of benefits. Furthermore, quantifying any resulting environmental benefits, such as reduced greenhouse gas emissions, or assessing the extent to which these benefits exceed the costs associated with developing these new high-speed rail routes is difficult. Some evaluations have been conducted in Spain and France and have indicated that net benefits were less than expected due to higher costs and lower than expected ridership, although, in France, the evaluations still found acceptable financial and social rates of return.[55]

Policies that provide incentives to shift passenger and freight traffic to rail offer the opportunity to attain a range of benefits simultaneously, but a variety of complicating factors can have a significant impact on the extent to which these benefits may be attained. In addition, if these policies are unable to generate the ridership or demand necessary to shift traffic from other modes to rail, the potential benefits may be further limited. While officials from some European countries we visited indicated that they have attained benefits from policies intended to shift traffic to rail, gains have been mixed, and the extent of benefits attained has depended on the specific context of policy implementation in each location, as the benefits realized are directly related to the particulars of each project. Furthermore, it is not always clear that the policy goals were feasible to begin with or that mode shift would have been the most cost-effective way to achieve the benefits sought. Some officials and stakeholders we met with told us that it is very difficult to attribute causation and draw conclusions regarding the effectiveness of transportation policy tools because so many factors are at play and may change simultaneously. In some cases, officials cannot determine the full extent of benefits or link impacts to a given policy with certainty, making it difficult for decision makers to know what to expect from future policies being considered or developed.

In the next section, we look at two recent U.S. investment programs that awarded grant funding to freight and intercity passenger rail projects. Although neither of these programs were adopted for the specific purpose of shifting passenger or freight traffic to rail, both programs do seek to attain benefits, such an economic development and environmental benefits, by investing in rail. As previously noted, the degree to which benefits can be generated depends on a variety of factors, including the ability to attract riders or freight shipments either through mode shift or new demand. We discuss

how applicants assessed the potential benefits and costs of their specific projects, based on the particular circumstances of each project, and the usefulness of those assessments for federal decision makers in making their investment decisions.

GRANT APPLICANTS' ASSESSMENTS OF PROJECT BENEFITS AND COSTS ARE OF VARYING QUALITY AND USEFULNESS TO DECISION MAKERS

Grant Applicants' Assessments of Project Benefits and Costs Were Not Comprehensive in Many Respects

According to DOT officials from both programs, as well as our assessment of 40 randomly selected rail-related TIGER and HSIPR applications,[56] information on project benefits and costs submitted by applicants to the TIGER and HSIPR[57] programs varied in both quality and comprehensiveness. While a small number of analyses of project benefits and costs were analytically strong—with sophisticated numerical projections of both benefits and costs and detailed information on their data and methodology—many others (1) did not quantify or monetize benefits to the extent possible, (2) did not appropriately account for benefits and costs, (3) omitted certain costs, and (4) did not include information on data limitations, methodologies for estimating benefits and costs, and uncertainties and assumptions underlying their analyses.

First, the majority of applications we assessed contained primarily qualitative discussion of project benefits, such as potential reductions in emissions, fuel consumption, or roadway congestion, which could have been quantified and monetized. For instance, while 36 of the 40 applications we assessed included qualitative information regarding potential reductions in congestion, 20 provided quantitative assessments of these benefits, and 13 provided monetary estimates.[58] This pattern was consistent across categories of benefits we assessed; however, some categories of impacts, such as safety and economic development, were even less frequently quantified. While federal guidelines, including Executive Order No. 12893, allow for discussion of benefits in a qualitative manner, they note the importance of quantifying and monetizing benefits to the maximum extent practicable. However, in some cases, certain categories of impacts may be more difficult to quantify than others and qualitative information on potential benefits and costs can be useful to decision makers.

Second, common issues identified by DOT economists in the applications they assessed[59] included failure to discount future benefits and costs to present values or failure to use appropriate discount rates,[60] double counting of benefits, and presenting costs only for the portion of the project accounted for in the application while presenting benefits for the full project. Similarly, 33 of the 40 applications we assessed did not use discount rates as recommended in OMB Circular No. A-94 and OMB Circular No. A-4. Further, DOT economists who reviewed assessments of project benefits and costs contained in selected TIGER applications stated that many applicants submitted economic impact analyses—which are generally used to assess how economic impacts would be distributed throughout an economy but not for conducting benefit-cost analysis of policy alternatives. Economic impact analyses may contain information that does not factor into calculations of net benefits, such as tax revenue and induced jobs, and do not generally include information on other key benefits that would be accounted for in a benefit-cost analysis, such as emissions reduction or congestion relief. Applicants' focus on economic impacts in their assessments of project benefits may have stemmed from additional funding criteria that DOT identified for both programs related to job creation and economic stimulus, as well as decision makers' focus on these issues at the state and local levels.

Third, important costs were often omitted from applications. In many cases, applicants would estimate a benefit, but not account for associated costs, such as increased noise, emissions, or potential additional accidents from new rail service. For instance, applicants often counted emission reduction benefits from mode shift to rail as a benefit but did not include corresponding increases in emissions from increased rail capacity and operation in their calculations of net benefits. Our assessments of TIGER and HSIPR applications found that of the applicants who projected potential safety or environmental benefits for their projects, only three applicants addressed potential safety costs, and only four applicants addressed potential environmental costs.

Finally, we also found that analyses of benefits and costs in many applications consistently lacked other key data and methodological information that federal guidelines such as OMB Circular No. A-94 and OMB Circular No. A-4 recommend should be accounted for in analyses of project benefits and costs.[61] Notably, the majority of the applications to the TIGER and HSIPR programs that we reviewed did not provide information related to uncertainty in projections, data limitations, and the assumptions underlying their models. While a small number of applications we assessed provided information in all of these areas, 31 of 40 did not provide information on the uncertainty associated with their estimates of benefits and costs, 28 out of 40 did not provide information on the models or other calculations used to arrive at estimates of benefits and costs, and 36 out of 40 did not provide information on the strengths and limitations of data used in their projections. Furthermore, of those that did provide information in these areas, the information was generally not comprehensive in nature. For example, multiple applications provided information on the models or calculations used to quantify or monetize benefits, but did not do so for all the benefit and cost calculations included in their analysis.

Short Time Frames, a Lack of Clear Standard Values, and Data Limitations Contributed to the Inconsistent Quality and Limited Usefulness of Assessments of Project Benefits and Costs

Applicants, industry experts, and DOT officials we spoke with reported that numerous challenges related to performing assessments of the benefits and costs of intercity passenger or freight rail projects can contribute to variation in the quality of assessments of project benefits and costs in applications to federal programs such as the TIGER and HSIPR programs. These challenges include (1) limited time, resources, and expertise for performing assessments of project benefits and costs; (2) a lack of clear guidance on standard values to use in the estimation of project benefits; and (3) limitations in data quality and access. These challenges impacted the usefulness of the information provided for decision makers, and, as a result, changes have been made or are being considered for future rounds of funding.

Time, Resources, and Expertise

Performing a comprehensive assessment of a proposed project's potential benefits and costs is time and resource intensive and requires significant expertise. According to experts, a detailed and comprehensive benefit-cost analysis requires careful analysis and may call for specialized data collection in order to develop projections of benefits and costs. The short time frames for assembling applications for the TIGER and HSIPR programs—which were designed to award funds quickly in order to provide economic stimulus—may have contributed to the poor quality of many assessments. In addition, according to DOT officials, many applicants to the TIGER and HSIPR programs may not have understood what information to include in their analyses. The recent nature of federal requirements for state rail planning means that states are still building their capacity to perform complex analyses to assess rail projects and, in many cases, rail divisions within state departments of transportation are very small. State rail divisions often face funding and manpower issues since there is typically no dedicated state funding for rail services, and state transportation planning has historically focused more on highway projects.[62] As a result, some applicants to competitive federal grant programs may have more capacity to perform assessments of project benefits and costs than others. For example, according to DOT officials, freight railroads have more resources to devote to developing models and estimating potential project benefits and costs.

Valuing Benefits

Standard values to monetize some benefits are not yet fully established, which can create inconsistency in the values used by applicants in their projections. While DOT has published guidance on standard estimates for the value of travel time and the value of a statistical life—which can be used to estimate the value of congestion mitigation efforts and safety improvements, respectively—values for other benefits are less clear. For instance, according to DOT officials, uncertainties associated with analyzing the value of time for freight shipment prevents DOT from issuing specific guidance in this area. In addition, there are substantial uncertainties associated with analyzing the value of many benefits, such as reduction in greenhouse gas emissions. While mode shift to rail may reduce pollution and greenhouse gas emissions, experts do not agree on the value to place on that benefit.[63] DOT has issued guidance on values for use in calculating the social benefits of pollutant emissions, however according to modeling experts we interviewed, disagreement regarding how to value different benefits can lead some analysts to limit their assessments of benefits and costs to only that which can be monetized, while others may include all categories of benefits and costs in their assessment. As a result, some TIGER and HSIPR applicants may have used differing values to monetize projected benefits and costs, while others did not monetize benefits at all. Without clear guidance to applicants on preferred values for use in assessments of project benefits and costs, DOT decision makers may be hindered in their ability to compare the results of assessments of benefits and costs across projects or across modes. A standard set of values for key benefit categories may enable transportation officials to more readily compare projects and potentially place more weight on the results of assessments of project benefits and costs in their decision-making processes.

Data Quality and Access

According to DOT officials, historically lower levels of state and federal funding for rail compared with other modes of transportation have contributed to data gaps that impact the ability of applicants to project benefits and costs for both intercity passenger rail and freight rail projects. For instance, lack of data on intercity passenger travel demand made it difficult for some applicants to the HSIPR program to quantify potential benefits for some new high-speed rail lines. The lack of data may be related to cuts to federal funding for the Bureau of Transportation Statistics resulting in a decreased emphasis on the collection of rail-related data. Multiple state and association officials stated that previous state and national surveys of travel behavior did not capture traveler purposes for intercity travel and did not have a sufficient number of intercity traveler responses for use in travel modeling. In addition, lack of access to proprietary data on goods movement made it challenging for some applicants to the TIGER program to quantify benefits that might be associated with freight rail. According to officials from the California Department of Transportation (Caltrans), when performing analyses to estimate project benefits and costs, Caltrans employees had to manually count freight trains for a 24-hour period in order to gather data for use in their analyses. Furthermore, state transportation officials we spoke with indicated that the quality of data available for use in projecting benefits and costs of a project is often inconsistent. Officials we interviewed stated that data included in assessments of project benefits and costs are often from different years, contain sampling error, and may be insufficient for their intended use. These limitations lessen the reliability of estimates produced to inform transportation decision-making, as available data provide critical inputs for travel models.

Modeling and forecasting limitations also make it harder to project shifts in transportation demand and related benefits and costs accurately. Benefit-cost analyses of transportation projects depend on forecasts of projected levels of usage, such as passenger rail ridership or potential freight shipments, in order to inform calculation of benefits and costs. Limitations of current models and data make it difficult to predict changes in traveler behavior, changes in warehousing and shipper behaviors for businesses, land use, or usage of nearby roads or alternative travel options that may result from a rail project. Since transportation demand modeling depends on information on traveler or shipper preferences in order to inform predictions, the lack of good intercity traveler and shipper demand data greatly impacts the quality of projections, particularly for new intercity passenger or freight rail service where no prior data exists to inform demand projections.

Usefulness of Assessments of Benefits and Costs

As a result of the limitations described above, DOT officials stated that the assessments of benefits and costs provided by TIGER and HSIPR applicants were less useful to decision makers than anticipated. In general, the majority of rail-related applications we reviewed that were forwarded for additional consideration for the TIGER program[64] contained assessments of project benefits and costs that were either marginally useful or not useful to DOT officials in their efforts to determine whether project benefits were likely to exceed project costs.[65] Overall, 62 percent of forwarded rail-related applications had assessments of benefits and costs that were rated by DOT economists as "marginally useful" or "not useful," and 38 percent had assessments that were rated as "very useful" or "useful" (see figure 4). However, DOT officials noted that railroads generally did a better job with their benefit-cost analyses in their applications than other modes.

While applicants to the HSIPR program were not required to conduct a benefit-cost analysis, the *Federal Register* notice for the program stated that information on benefits and costs provided by applicants would be used by DOT to conduct a comprehensive benefit-cost analysis for projects. However, according to FRA officials, the quality of the information provided prevented DOT from being able to use the information in this manner.

While it is possible to offset the impact of the limitations described above and improve the usefulness of assessments of benefits and costs to decision makers by providing clear information on assumptions and uncertainty within analyses, as we stated above, very few TIGER and HSIPR applicants did so. Without information on projection methodologies and assumptions, DOT officials were not able to consistently determine how demand and benefit-cost projections were developed and whether the projections were reasonable. As a result, officials for both programs focused on simply determining whether project benefits were likely to exceed project costs, rather than a more detailed assessment of the magnitude of projects' benefits and costs in relation to one another. See app. IV for a discussion of the challenges related to assumptions and uncertainty we encountered during our attempt to use a model to predict freight mode shift from truck to rail.

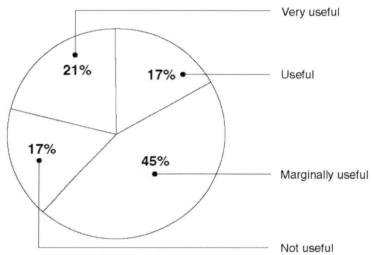

Source: GAO analysis of DOT data.

Note: DOT economists assessed usefulness of benefit-cost information only for those applications that were forwarded by initial DOT review teams for additional consideration.

Figure 4. DOT Assessment of Usefulness of Benefit-Cost Analyses from Forwarded Rail-Related TIGER Applications.

The varying quality and focus of assessments of project benefits and costs included in both TIGER and HSIPR applications resulted in additional work for DOT officials in order for DOT to be able to determine whether project benefits were likely to exceed project costs. For example, DOT officials stated that DOT economists for the TIGER program spent 3 to 4 hours per application examining whether it contained any improper analysis techniques or other weaknesses, seeking missing information, and resolving issues in the analyses. For the HSIPR program, a DOT economist with subject matter expertise reviewed the demand forecasts provided by selected Track 2 applicants,[66] devoting significant time to assess the level of risk the uncertainty in these projections was likely to pose to the ultimate success of the project.

Recent Changes and Improvements to Program Guidance

In order to improve the quality of applicant assessments of project benefits and costs, DOT economists identified limitations of the benefit-cost analyses submitted during TIGER I and used that information to develop guidance for TIGER II.[67] In the *Federal Register* notice for TIGER II, DOT provided additional information to applicants regarding what should be included in assessments of project benefits and costs.[68] This guidance included information on the differences between benefit-cost analysis and economic impact analysis, assessment of alternatives in relation to a baseline, discounting, forecasting, transparency and reproducibility of calculations, and methods of calculating various benefits and costs. As part of its guidance on assessing costs, DOT noted that applicants should use life-cycle cost analysis in estimating the costs of projects.[69] For example, DOT guidance states that external costs, such as noise, increased congestion, and environmental pollutants resulting from construction or other project activities, should be included as costs in applicants' analyses. Furthermore, applicants should include, to the extent possible, other costs caused during construction, such as delays and increased vehicle operating costs.

FRA also plans to alter HSIPR requirements in order to increase the quality of information on project benefits and costs provided by future applicants. According to FRA officials, while applicants to the second round of HSIPR funding were presented with similar guidelines for assessing project benefits and costs as those provided in the first round, future HSIPR applicants will be required to provide more rigorous projections of ridership, benefits, and costs and to revise their assessments of project benefits and costs based on their improved ridership projections. Officials noted, however, that the process will be iterative and anticipated that models for the high-speed rail program will improve as domestic historical data on ridership becomes available over time. In addition, officials stated that FRA plans to take steps to encourage consistency in the methodologies grant applicants use to project demand, benefits, and costs. For instance, FRA is currently in the preliminary stages of developing a benefit-cost framework for states and localities, which represent the majority of applicants to programs such as TIGER and HSIPR, to use in assessing rail projects. Officials stated that FRA plans to issue guidance on performing assessments of benefits and costs for passenger rail projects when the framework is fully developed but did not provide a timeline for its development.

While DOT officials for both programs have taken steps to improve the quality of benefit-cost information and associated analyses in the short term, other steps are necessary to improve quality over time. Some of these additional steps, such as developing historical data for intercity passenger rail demand, making improvements to forecasting and modeling, and increasing accessibility and quality of key data, may take more time. Nonetheless, improving the quality of benefit and cost information considered for programs such as TIGER and HSIPR could simplify the decision-making process and lend more credence to the merit of the projects ultimately selected for funding.

CONCLUSIONS

Difficult and persistent problems face the U.S. transportation system today. Our system is largely powered by vehicles that use fossil fuels that produce harmful air emissions and contribute to climate change. Our existing infrastructure is aging and, in many places, is in a poor state of repair. Demand for freight and passenger travel will continue to grow, and the growing congestion in urban areas and at key bottlenecks in the system costs Americans billions of dollars in wasted time, fuel, and productivity each year. Adding to these problems, expanding or improving the efficiency of our existing road and air transportation networks has proven difficult, costly, and time-consuming. Both the HSIPR and TIGER programs provided a new opportunity to invest in rail—a mode that has historically been underrepresented in the U.S. transportation funding framework. Some see investment in rail infrastructure, along with other policies designed to shift traffic to rail, as important to addressing these problems, pointing to rail's advantages over cars and freight trucks in terms of energy efficiency, safety, and lower emissions. While investments in rail or policies designed to shift traffic to rail may generate some benefits—as occurred to some degree in the United Kingdom and Germany—benefits must be weighed against direct project costs and other costs (e.g., noise) to determine whether an investment or policy produces overall net benefits. Further, close attention must be paid to the extent to which freight and passenger travel can actually shift to rail from other modes, given the choices available to, and the preferences of, travelers and shippers.

While an assessment of benefits and costs is only one factor among many in decision making regarding these investments and policies, a decision maker's ability to weigh information depends on the quality of benefit and cost information provided by project sponsors—regardless of whether this information is provided in a benefit-cost analysis or a more general discussion or enumeration of benefits and costs. We found that many TIGER and HSIPR applicants struggled to provide the benefit-cost information requested or to use appropriate values designated for their respective program. The lack of consistency and completeness in the benefit-cost information provided makes it more difficult for decision makers to conduct direct project comparisons or to fully understand the extent to which benefits are achievable and the trade-offs involved. While the shortened time frames of the programs and resource limitations among project sponsors were key causes of the varying quality of analyses, data limitations (including a lack of historical data—particularly with respect to high-speed rail), data inconsistencies, and data unavailability also accounted for some limitations in applicants' benefit-cost information and will continue to impact these analyses in future funding rounds. Until data quality, data gaps, and access issues are addressed for the data inputs needed for rail modeling and analysis, projections of rail benefits will continue to be of limited use. In addition, almost no applicants discussed limitations in their analysis, including the assumptions made and levels of uncertainty in their projections. Only when assumptions and uncertainty are conveyed in assessments of benefits and costs can decision makers determine the appropriate weight to give to certain projections.

To its credit, DOT has provided more explicit guidance to TIGER applicants in its second round of grant applications on how to meet federal benefit-cost analysis guidelines. While such guidance should result in improved quality of benefit-cost information provided for this program, this guidance neither ensures consistency across analyses in terms of common data sources, values, and models, nor will it have any impact on how benefits and costs are evaluated across programs that invest in other modes (such as the Federal-Aid Highway Program) which do not have a benefit-cost analysis requirement. Providing more standardized values for calculating project benefits and costs and developing a more consistent approach to assessing project benefits and costs so that proposed projects across modes may be more easily compared with one another can have numerous benefits. For instance, standardized values and a consistent approach allow for more confidence that projects and policies chosen will produce the greatest benefits relative to other alternatives, give more credence to investment decisions across programs and modes, and limit DOT officials' need to invest time and resources in order to use the information as part of the decision making process. If benefit-cost considerations are ever to play a greater role, DOT will need to look at ways it can improve the quality and consistency of the data available to project sponsors.

RECOMMENDATIONS FOR EXECUTIVE ACTION

To improve the data available to the Department of Transportation and rail project sponsors, we recommend that the Secretary of Transportation, in consultation with Congress and other stakeholders, take the following two actions:

- Conduct a data needs assessment and identify which data are needed to conduct cost-effective modeling and analysis for intercity rail, determine limitations to the data used for inputs, and develop a strategy to address these limitations. In doing so, DOT should identify barriers to accessing existing data, consider whether authorization for additional data collection for intercity rail travel is warranted, and determine which entities shall be responsible for generating or collecting needed data.
- Encourage effective decision making and enhance the usefulness of assessments of benefits and costs, for both intercity passenger and freight rail projects by providing ongoing guidance and training on developing benefit and cost information for rail projects and by providing more direct and consistent requirements for assessing benefits and costs across transportation funding programs. In doing so, DOT should:
  - Direct applicants to follow federal guidance outlined in both the Presidential Executive Order 12893 and OMB Circulars Nos. A-94 and A-4 in developing benefit and cost information.
  - Require applicants to clearly communicate their methodology for calculating project benefits and costs including information on assumptions underlying calculations, strengths and limitations of data used, and the level of uncertainty in estimates of project benefits and costs.
  - Ensure that applicants receive clear and consistent guidance on values to apply for key assumptions used to estimate potential project benefits and costs.

APPENDIX I. METHODOLOGY APPENDIX I: OBJECTIVES, SCOPE, AND METHODOLOGY

To better understand the potential net benefits of intercity passenger and freight rail, we examined (1) the extent to which transportation policy tools that provide incentives to shift passenger and freight traffic to rail may generate emissions, congestion, and economic development benefits and (2) how project benefits and costs are assessed for investment in intercity passenger and freight rail and how the strengths and limitations of these assessments impact federal decision making.

Interviews

We conducted interviews with the Department of Transportation (DOT), the Environmental Protection Agency (EPA), and Amtrak. We also interviewed representatives from transportation coalitions and associations, metropolitan planning organizations, state DOTs, and transportation consultants. Interviews with officials were in regards to methods to assess the benefits and costs of transportation investments and the limitations and challenges to assessing benefits. We also conducted interviews with officials from the High-Speed Intercity Passenger Rail (HSIPR), the Transportation Investment Generating Economic Recovery (TIGER), and Transportation Infrastructure Finance and Innovation Act (TIFIA) programs to gather insights into the usefulness of the cost-benefit study information in decision making. In addition to interviews with agency officials, interviews were conducted in three rail corridors (California, Midwest, and the Northeast) to ascertain additional information on challenges associated with conducting and communicating findings from benefit and cost assessments to decision makers. These interviews involved applicants and other corridor stakeholders who had applied to either or both the HSIPR and TIGER grant programs. Similarly, some of our interviews with organizations in the rail corridors included consultants such as Cambridge Systematics and Parsons Brinckerhoff which were involved in the development of studies for corridors. Following is table 3 with a list of selected organizations whose officials and representatives we interviewed.

Table 3. Interviews

Federal Agencies and Entities	Industry associations
Amtrak	American Association of State
DOT	Highway and Transportation Officials
Bureau of Transportation Statistics	American Public Transportation
Federal Highway Administration Federal	Association Association of American
Railroad Administration	Railroads
Inspector General	
Office of the Secretary	
EPA	
United States	**United Kingdom**
California Department of Transportation	Department for Transport
California High Speed Rail Authority	Greengauge 21
CSX	National Audit Office
I-95 Corridor Coalition	Network Rail
Illinois Department Of Transportation	Rail Freight Group
Metropolitan Transportation Commission	**Germany**
Northern New England Passenger Rail	Deustche Bahn
Authority	Federal Ministry of Environment,
Ohio Department of Transportation Ohio	Nature Conservation and Nuclear
Rail Development Commission	Safety
Pennsylvania Department of	Federal Ministry of Finance
Transportation	Federal Ministry of Transport,
San Diego Association of Governments	Building and Urban Development
Other	
Louis Thompson, Thompson, Galenson	
and Associates	
Organization for Economic Cooperation	
and Development (OECD), International	
Transport Forum	
University of Leeds, Institute for	
Transport Studies	

Source: GAO.

STUDY REVIEW

We reviewed our prior reports and documentation from an array of sources, including the DOT Inspector General, Congressional Research Service, and Congressional Budget Office. In addition, we identified studies through our interviews with stakeholders and conducted an extensive systematic search of literature published in the last 15 years. We reviewed this information to identify studies that analyzed the benefits and costs of intercity passenger and freight rail, mode shift to intercity passenger or freight rail, or the potential net benefits that could be attained through mode shift. In general, we did not find a sufficient number of available studies that adequately addressed our researchable questions, had an appropriate scope, or utilized empirically reliable methodologies. As a result, we used the studies and information we reviewed to inform the engagement as a whole and provided examples and illustrations of the potential costs and benefits that may be attained from policies that provide incentives to shift traffic to rail. In addition, we conducted case studies in the United Kingdom and Germany and asked officials to synthesize their experiences based on their professional judgment and data. Officials we met with also confirmed that it is difficult to causally link policy interventions to specific outcomes.

ASSESSMENT OF HSIPR AND TIGER APPLICATIONS' COST AND BENEFIT INFORMATION

We reviewed and assessed information on potential project benefits and costs included in selected applications to the HSIPR grant program and the Grants for TIGER grant program—20 applications from each grant program. We selected a nongeneralizable random sample of 40 applications from a larger pool of HSIPR and TIGER applications that we identified as including components related to intercity passenger rail or freight rail. For HSIPR, we included all applications submitted under Track 2 of the program, which focused on intercity passenger rail projects, in our selection pool, while for TIGER, we included all applications requesting more than $20 million that included components related to intercity passenger rail or freight rail in project descriptions provided by DOT. Twenty applications from each grant program were randomly selected for our review. The random sample of applications was weighted to ensure approximately proportional representation of applications from both programs that were awarded funding by DOT to those that were not awarded funding by DOT and, for the TIGER program, weighted to ensure approximately proportional representation of applications that were selected by DOT for additional review during DOT's application review process to those that were not selected by DOT for additional review.

Information pertaining to project benefits and costs in each of the 40 randomly selected applications was independently reviewed by two of our analysts based on Office of Management and Budget (OMB) guidelines for benefit-cost analysis and input from our economists and methodologists.

Application information assessed by our analysts included whether benefits and costs related to congestion mitigation, emissions reduction, and economic development were assessed qualitatively, quantitatively, or were monetized. In addition, analysts identified whether applications included information on a number of key methodological elements identified by OMB and in our prior work. Any discrepancies in findings by the two analysts were reconciled for the final assessment.

INTERNATIONAL CASE STUDIES: THE UNITED KINGDOM AND GERMANY

We conducted case studies of selected policies and programs in the United Kingdom and Germany to learn more about policies to address concerns about emissions, congestion and economic development. These two countries were chosen based on a number of criteria, including experience in implementing capacity enhancing and demand management policy tools in order to encourage mode shift to rail and attain potential benefits. We reviewed studies and reports on policy tools used in these countries and in the European Union. We interviewed officials from the United Kingdom's Department for Transport and Germany's Ministry of Transport, Building and Urban Development. In addition, we interviewed officials in the German Federal Ministry of Finance and Ministry for the Environment, Nature Conservation and Nuclear Safety, as well as the United Kingdom's National Audit Office. We also met with representatives from rail industry organizations and rail companies and stakeholder groups from these countries. For more information, see appendix II.

COMPUTER SIMULATIONS OF FREIGHT DIVERSION FROM TRUCK TO RAIL

We conducted our own simulation of transportation policy scenarios on mode choice for freight shipments. Disaggregated data from the Freight Analysis Framework (FAF)[70] was analyzed to obtain the distance traveled for shipments across commodity and truck types. Then this data from FAF, along with aggregated data on underlying assumptions, were used as inputs into the Intermodal Transportation and Inventory Cost Model (ITIC).[71] This model estimates mode choices for each shipment under baseline conditions and various policy scenarios. See appendix IV for additional discussion of the simulations.

We reviewed technical documentation associated with both of these models. We also conducted interviews with officials at DOT to better understand any data limitations or reliability issues with the model and data inputs. For more information see appendix IV.

APPENDIX II. INTERNATIONAL CASE STUDY SUMMARIES: THE UNITED KINGDOM AND GERMANY

The United Kingdom

Background

The United Kingdom's Department for Transport sets the strategic direction for the railways and Network Rail owns and operates Britain's rail infrastructure. Network Rail is a private corporation run by a board of directors and composed of approximately 100 members—some rail industry stakeholders and some members of the general public. Freight and passenger operators pay access charges to Network Rail for access to the rail tracks. In the United Kingdom, freight and passenger rail share many of the same tracks. The system is open to competition through passenger rail franchises and through "open access" provisions for freight and other new passenger services.

Transportation Project Planning Process

The Department for Transport's current approach to transportation policy planning emphasizes the assessment of a range of options driven by the desire to push transportation as a means to improve general economic performance, as well as environmental and societal goals. The Department for Transport plans and develops freight and intercity passenger rail projects based on a 5-year planning cycle, referred to as a Control Period. The last Control Period covering 2009-2014 resulted in plans to invest £6.6 billion (at 2010/2011 prices) in capacity enhancements for the passenger and freight rail system and strategic rail freight network. The 5-year cycle is intended to identify, develop, and prioritize policy interventions and investment decisions, reflecting the long-term nature of the transportation sector. The Department for Transport publishes High Level Output Specifications and Statements of Funds

Available, reflecting what types of rail projects the government wants to buy based on the government's transport goals and objectives and how much money it has to spend on those projects. Network Rail selects and implements projects to meet the High Level Output Specifications and outlines planned projects in a detailed delivery plan. All potential United Kingdom transportation projects are required to undergo standardized assessment processes to evaluate benefits and costs through the Web-based Transport Appraisal Guidance, which includes guidance on benefit-cost analysis for major transportation projects, including information on comparisons of proposed projects to alternatives, data sources for use in analyses, and methods for quantifying benefits and costs and performing sensitivity analysis.

Selected Policy Tools

The Department for Transport has developed and implemented a range of policies to encourage a shift to rail transport. We explored some of these policies—in figure 5 below—during our site visits in the United Kingdom.

Country	Selected policies	Type of rail	
		Intercity passenger	Freight
United Kingdom 	Recent and planned high-speed rail projects	✓	
	Mode shift revenue support scheme		✓
	Freight facilities grants		✓

Sources: GAO and Map Resources (map).

Figure 5. Selected Polices to Benefit Intercity Passenger and Freight Rail in the United Kingdom.

Recent and planned high-speed rail projects (HS1 and HS2)—The Channel Tunnel Rail Link—referred to as HS1—is the United Kingdom portion of the route used by the Eurostar services from London to Paris and Brussels and was completed in 2007. The 109-kilometer Channel Tunnel Rail Link was the first major new railway to be constructed in the United Kingdom for over a century and the first high-speed railway. In 2009, the government began to develop plans for a new dedicated high-speed passenger rail line— HS2. The current government plans to begin a formal consultation process in 2011 and hopes to begin construction on the new high-speed line by 2015.

Mode shift revenue support scheme—This program provides funding to companies for operating costs associated with shipping via rail or inland water freight instead of road. It is intended to facilitate and support modal shift, as well as generating environmental and wider social benefits from having fewer freight shipments on Britain's roads.

Freight facilities grants—These grants provide support for freight infrastructure capital projects such as rail sidings or loading and unloading equipment. Funding is granted on the principle that if the facilities were not provided, the freight in question would go by road. Applicants must predict the type and quantity of goods that will use the proposed facility and demonstrate that the freight facility will secure the removal of freight trucks from specific routes. The program has been available since the 1970s, and it has a long history of providing funding for capital infrastructure.

Germany

Background

In Germany, the Federal Ministry of Transport, Building and Urban Development (Ministry of Transport) is responsible for financing the development and maintenance of the country's intercity passenger and freight rail network. Germany has the largest rail network in Europe, and both the intercity passenger and freight rail systems are open to competition. The majority of the rail system in Germany is managed by a single infrastructure provider—Deutsche Bahn.[72] The German government provides Deutsche Bahn with approximately €3.9 billion a year in investment grants for infrastructure renewal, upgrades, and new projects; freight and passenger operators pay access charges to Deutsche Bahn for access to the rail tracks. In addition to serving as the railway infrastructure provider, Deutsche Bahn also provides much of the intercity passenger and freight logistics service in Germany. Passenger and freight rail usually share the same track in Germany which, according to German transport officials, can enhance the efficiency of the network. However, sharing the same network also impacts the overall capacity available to accommodate new passenger or freight traffic.

Transportation Project Planning Process

The Ministry of Transport develops a Federal Transport Infrastructure Master Plan approximately every 10 years to set the long-term strategic policy direction for both passenger and freight transportation. These infrastructure plans describe projects required to cope with the forecast traffic development. The goals and objectives of these long-term plans are then translated into 5-year plans—Federal Transport Infrastructure Action Plans—which are then used to develop new projects. After determining short-term transportation priorities and developing action plans intended to align with long-term goals, all potential rail projects undergo standardized assessment processes to evaluate benefits and costs. As the primary infrastructure manager for the rail network in Germany, Deutsche Bahn maintains rail data sets that allow officials to generate consistent estimates of project benefits and costs with confidence, facilitated by centralized data collection. The rail infrastructure planning process is currently under way, and officials at the Ministry of Transport have just reviewed requirement plans for rail infrastructures projects—a process that occurs every 5 years—in order to complete and release an updated Action Plan.

Selected Policy Tools

Germany's Ministry of Transport has developed and implemented a range of policies that may encourage a shift to rail transport. We explored some of these policies—in figure 6 below—during our site visits in Germany.

Country	Selected policies	Type of rail	
		Intercity passenger	Freight
Germany 	Upgrade and maintain high-speed rail network	✓	
	Vehicle mineral oil (fuel) tax	✓	✓
	Heavy Goods Vehicle tolls		✓

Sources: GAO and Map Resources (map).

Figure 6. Selected Polices to Benefit Intercity Passenger and Freight Rail in Germany.

Upgrade and maintain the rail network—The German government has committed to investing annually in projects to upgrade and renew the existing high-speed and passenger rail network. Each year, the German government invests approximately €3.9 billion to renew the existing rail infrastructure and to construct, upgrade, or extend rail infrastructure.

Vehicle mineral oil (fuel) tax—Between 1999 and 2003, the German government began to implement routine, annual increases in the vehicle fuel tax for the explicit purpose of curbing car use and promoting the purchase of more fuel-efficient vehicles. Diesel is now taxed at approximately 47 euro cents a liter, and gas is taxed at 65 euro cents a liter, generating approximately €39 billion in revenue in 2009 for the general tax fund.

Heavy Goods Vehicle (HGV) tolls—Germany implemented a distance-based HGV toll in 2005, in part to support an explicit goal of shifting a portion of freight traffic to rail. The policy generated approximately €4.4 billion revenue in 2009, which was primarily used to maintain and upgrade the road network.[73] This policy was viewed as imposing additional costs on the business community, and the new government has said it will not raise the toll rates or expand the tax to passenger vehicles in this legislative period.

APPENDIX III. HSIPR AND DISCRETIO DISCRETIONARY GRANT PROGRAM INFORMATION

HSIPR

The American Reinvestment and Recovery Act of 2009 (Recovery Act)[74] provided $8 billion to develop high-speed and intercity passenger rail service, funding the Passenger Rail Investments and Improvement Act (PRIIA), which was enacted in October 2008.[75] The funding made available is significantly more money than Congress provided to fund rail in recent years. The Federal Railroad Administration (FRA) launched the high-speed and intercity passenger rail (HSIPR) program in June 2009 with the issuance of a notice of funding availability and interim program guidance, which outlined the requirements and procedures for obtaining federal funds.[76] Congress appropriated an additional $2.5 billion for high-speed rail for fiscal year 2010,[77] and in January 2010 FRA announced the selection of 62 projects in 23 states and the District of Columbia.

FRA allowed applicants to the HSIPR program to submit applications to be evaluated under four funding tracks.[78] See table 4 below.

Applications were evaluated by technical evaluation panels against three categories of criteria: (1) public return on investment across categories of benefits including transportation benefits, economic recovery benefits, and other public benefits; (2) project success factors, such as project management approach and sustainability of benefits, as assessed by adequacy of engineering, proposed project schedule, National Environmental Policy Act compliance, and thoroughness of management plan; and (3) other attributes, such as timeliness of project completion. Projects were rated on a scale of 1 point to 5 points, with 1 point being the lowest, and 5 points being the highest, based on the fulfillment of objectives for each separate criterion.

Using the best available tools, applicants were required to include benefit and cost information for the following three general categories of benefits:

- Transportation benefits, which include improved intercity passenger service, improved transportation network integration, and safety benefits;
- Economic recovery, which includes preserving and creating jobs (particularly in economically distressed areas); and
- Other public benefits, such as environmental quality, energy efficiency, and livable communities.

Table 4. High-Speed Intercity Passenger Rail Program Funding Tracks

Track 1	Applications aimed at addressing the economic recovery goals of the Recovery Act through construction of ready-to-go intercity passenger rail projects, including projects to relieve congestion.
Track 2	Applications that included projects either to develop new high-speed rail corridors and intercity passenger rail services or substantially upgrade existing corridor services, excluding intercity passenger rail congestion projects.
Track 3	Applications that focused on service planning activities. These projects are aimed at establishing a pipeline of future high-speed rail and intercity passenger rail projects and service development programs by advancing planning activities for applicants at earlier stages of the development process.
Track 4	Provides an alternative for projects that would otherwise fit under Track 1, but applicants must offer at least a 50% nonfederal share of financing. Applicants have up to 5 years (as opposed to 2 years) to complete projects.

Source: HSIPR *Federal Register* notice.

Final project selections were made by the FRA Administrator building upon the work of the technical evaluation panels and applying four selection criteria specified in the *Federal Register* notice: (1) region/location, including regional balance across the country and balance among large and small population centers; (2) innovation, including pursuit of new technology and promotion of domestic manufacturing; (3) partnerships, including multistate agreements; and (4) tracks and round timing, including project schedules and costs.

TIGER

The Recovery Act also appropriated $1.5 billion for discretionary grants to be administered by DOT for capital investments in the nation's surface transportation infrastructure.[79] These grants were available on a competitive basis to fund transportation projects that would preserve and create jobs and provide long-term benefits, as well as incorporate innovation and promote public-private or other partnership approaches. In making awards, the legislation required DOT to address several statutory priorities, including achieving an equitable geographic distribution of the funds, balancing the needs of urban and rural communities, prioritizing projects for which a TIGER grant would complete a package of funding, and others.[80] In December 2009 Congress appropriated $600 million to DOT for a "TIGER II" discretionary grant program, which was similar to the TIGER program's structure and objectives.[81]

Eligible projects included highway or bridge projects, public transportation, passenger and freight rail projects, and port infrastructure projects. The TIGER program established three categories of project applications based on the amount of federal funding sought[82] and three sets of criteria to determine grant awards in each project application category:

- *Primary selection criteria:* Long-term outcomes, such as state of good repair, evidence of long-term benefits, livability, sustainability, safety, and job creation and economic stimulus.
- *Secondary selection criteria:* Priority to projects that use innovative strategies to pursue long-term outcomes and those that demonstrate strong collaboration among a broad range of participants. Secondary

  selection criteria were weighted less than primary selection criteria in the application review process.
- *Program-specific criteria:* Program-specific information was used as a tie breaker to differentiate between similar projects. This information was only applied to projects in the following categories: bridge replacement, transit projects, TIGER-TIFIA payment projects, and port infrastructure projects.

APPENDIX IV. COMPUTER SIMULATIONS OF FREIGHT DIVERSION FROM TRUCK TO RAIL

In general, quantifying benefits that may be attained through rail can be challenging, in part, because of data limitations. In order to both estimate the extent to which freight shipments might be diverted from truck to rail under various scenarios and identify challenges related to making such estimates, we conducted simulations using a computer model developed by DOT. We sought to estimate the number of diverted truck freight shipments under scenarios that increased the price or decreased the speed of freight shipments by truck as compared with rail.

ITIC Model

The Intermodal Transportation Inventory Cost (ITIC) model is a computer model for calculating the costs associated with shipping freight via alternative modes, namely truck and rail. The model can be used to perform policy analysis of issues concerning long-haul freight movement, such as diversion of freight shipments from truck to rail.[83] DOT provides the ITIC model framework as a useful tool for ongoing policy studies, and shares the model, along with some internally developed data, for this purpose. We chose to use the ITIC model to simulate mode shift from truck to rail because of its federal origins and its direct applicability to freight shipments.[84]

The ITIC model—of which we used the highway freight to rail intermodal version—predicts diversion from truck to rail by assuming that shippers will select the mode of transportation with lower total shipment cost. The model replicates the decision-making trade-offs made by shippers in selecting which transportation mode to use for freight shipments. The model estimates the total cost—including both transportation and logistics costs—required to ship freight by both truck and rail for a given type of commodity and a given county-to-county route. Transportation costs include the costs associated with the actual movement of commodities, such as loading and unloading freight, and logistics costs represent a range of other costs, such as loss and damage of the freight, safety stock carrying cost, and capital cost on claims (see figure 8 for the components of these costs).

In order to estimate diversions of freight shipments from truck to rail, the ITIC model runs in two steps. First, the model establishes a baseline that can be used for comparison against each of the simulated scenarios. To do this, the ITIC model requires input data on actual truck freight shipments that it uses to calculate total cost to ship each type of commodity for each county-to-county pair for both truck and rail. After generating a base case, diversion of freight from truck to rail can be estimated for various scenarios by changing the input assumptions to the model. As these assumptions are changed, the model reestimates the transportation and logistics costs for both truck and rail and determines whether these estimated changes have made rail a lower cost option for any of the shipments that were originally sent by truck. The model assumes that shipments will switch from truck to rail if the total cost for making a shipment by rail is lower than the total costs for making a shipment by truck.

Reliability of Model Inputs

A lack of reliable data for a number of major ITIC model inputs at the national level prevented us from fully assessing the uncertainty associated with estimates of freight diversion from truck to rail. As a result, we are unable to report on the confidence levels of the results of our simulations. The ITIC model is based on 26 inputs (see table 6 for a complete list of ITIC model inputs). For our national analysis, empirical data were available for 9 of the inputs; accordingly, we had to rely on the preprogrammed model assumptions for the remaining 17 inputs.[85] Using these 26 inputs, the model made 24 calculations (see table 7 for full list of ITIC model calculations), 22 of which relied on at least one of the model's 17 default assumptions (see table 5 below).

Table 5. Extent of Data and Assumptions Underlying Intermodal Transportation Inventory Cost Model Inputs and Calculations

	ITIC components	**Number**
ITIC model inputs	Assumptions	17
	Data	9
Total		**26**
ITIC model calculations	Calculated from assumptions	22
	Calculated only from data	2
Total		**24**

Source: GAO analysis of ITIC model.

To determine whether the available data and model assumptions were reliable for our purposes, we considered some important factors for assessing data reliability, including their relevance, completeness, accuracy, validity, and consistency.[86] We found that the data and the basis for assumptions used in the ITIC model vary in terms of the following factors.

- Relevance: The 26 ITIC model inputs are relevant for the purposes of determining total transportation and logistics costs. These inputs have been shown to be conceptually important because they reflect economic theory underlying shipper choices, include a range of factors specified in the literature on freight shipments, and provide default assumptions based on theory and professional expertise.
- Completeness: Completeness refers to the extent that relevant records are present and the fields in each record are populated appropriately. We were unable to obtain complete national data for 20 ITIC model inputs. Of these 20 inputs, partial data were available for 3.[87] For the remaining 17 inputs, we were unable to obtain any empirical data and consequently relied on the default assumptions that are provided in the model itself. However, without a reliable source of available data against which to judge the accuracy and validity of these assumed values, we could not determine how much uncertainty the assumptions added to any estimates produced by the model.
- Accuracy: Accuracy refers to the extent that recorded data reflect the actual underlying information. Of the 26 ITIC model inputs, we were unable to verify the accuracy for 20, including all 17 assumptions, as well as available truck rate data and 2 inputs (weight per cubic foot and value per pound of each commodity group) provided by FRA. FRA officials stated that they originally generated these input values using empirical data, but were unable to provide documentation of their analysis. We were therefore unable to judge the accuracy of the resulting data, or the level of uncertainty associated with estimates produced from FRA's data.
- Validity: Validity refers to an input correctly representing what it is supposed to measure. Of the 26 ITIC model inputs, we were unable to verify the validity for 18, including all 17 default assumptions and available truck rate data. For the latter, we used the source of data previously used by the Federal Highway Administration, a proprietary collection of truck rates from 2006 for 120 city pairs. Documentation of the collection methods was unavailable, and we were not able to

validate or assess the data for reliability, and thus could not estimate the uncertainty associated with per-mile truck rates. Because this value is a primary driver of total transportation and logistics costs, the uncertain reliability of truck rate data was a major limitation to using the model's estimates.

- Consistency: Consistency is a subcategory of accuracy and refers to the need to obtain and use data that are clear and well defined enough to yield similar results in similar analyses. Of the 26 ITIC model inputs, we identified consistency issues for 7 data inputs. For example, truck rate data were collected in 2006, and data on truck shipments were from 2002, making it problematic to compare these figures. For the other 6 inputs, we encountered different levels of data aggregation for data that we had otherwise deemed reliable. For example, the FAF collects regional data, while the FRA lookup tables for certain truck and rail origin and destination miles are collected at a county level. In order to use both sources of data, the FAF data had to be disaggregated for use at the county level, and our disaggregation method adds additional uncertainty to our estimates.

Reliability of Model Estimates

In order to better understand the impact of uncertainty in the ITIC model's estimates caused by use of assumptions and data of questionable reliability, we examined how the model's estimates change when key underlying assumptions were varied. In particular, we used the model to simulate the impact that a 50-cent increase in per-mile truck rates would have on vehicle miles traveled (VMT) under two scenarios: the first scenario uses the model's default values for all assumptions, including truck speeds of 50 miles per hour, freight loss and damage as a percentage of gross revenue equal to 0.07 percent, and a reliability factor equal to 0.4;[88] the second scenario changes these three assumptions to respective values of 40 miles per hour, 0.10 percent freight loss and damage, and reliability factor equal to 0.5. Each of these changes creates a higher total cost for trucks, potentially leading the model to predict some additional diversion to rail. However, for these sensitivity analyses, we are more concerned with the impact of changing truck rates under the alternative scenarios than we are with the individual impacts of changing assumptions.

For a 50-cent increase (approximately 30 percent of per mile truck rates) in the first scenario, the model estimates a reduction in VMT of about 1.02

percent. For the same reduction in rates in the second scenario, the model estimates a reduction in VMT of about 1.04 percent. Figure 7 shows the estimated percentage reduction in VMT associated with increased per-mile truck rates for the two scenarios. Under either scenario, the impact of increasing per-mile truck rates by approximately 30 percent results in decreases of roughly 1 percent of VMT. This result suggests that we can have some degree of confidence that the model will consistently predict that changing per-mile truck rates will have a minor impact on total VMT traveled.

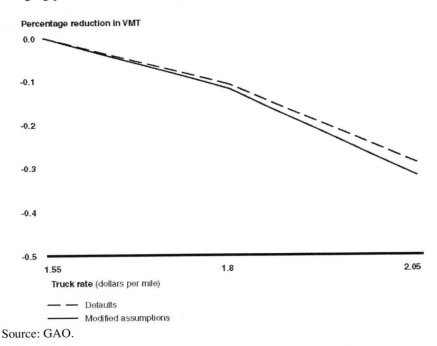

Source: GAO.

Figure 7. Impact of Increased Per-Mile Truck Rates on Vehicle Miles Traveled (VMT) by Trucks under Two Scenarios.

In spite of the results of our two scenarios, the estimates of VMT diversion based on the ITIC model are still subject to limitations. As a result, these estimates are only suggestive, rather than conclusive, of the impact that an increase in per-mile truck rates might have on VMT reduction in actual policy scenarios. First, the issues of completeness, accuracy, validity, and consistency of our data negatively impact their reliability and increase the uncertainty of our estimates. Second, because of resource constraints, our analysis only varies 3 of the 17 default ITIC model assumptions and considers only one change in these values, instead of varying a larger number of assumptions for a wider range of scenarios (see table 6 for a full list of assumptions). Therefore, we cannot conclude that the model results are robust to all plausible variations in all of the model assumptions. Therefore, while the results of our simulation suggest that a 50-cent increase in per-mile truck rates would have a limited impact on diversion of freight from truck to rail in the short-term, we do not have enough confidence in the quality of data inputs to make precise predictions that would be reliable enough to inform policymaking decisions. Reliable data for model inputs would be necessary in order to produce estimates of changes in VMT with confidence.

Implications for Future Simulations

Sufficiently reliable data were not readily available for producing national estimates of mode shift under specific policy scenarios. As a result, it was necessary to rely on assumptions and data of undetermined reliability when conducting national simulations, which may result in unreliable estimates of freight diversion and an inability to fully quantify the uncertainty of the estimates produced. Our simulations suggest that a large increase (approximately 30 percent) in per-mile truck rates results could result in a relatively small (approximately 1 percent) decrease in VMT, even when multiple assumptions related to truck freight cost are changed. Despite this, limitations in the reliability of our data and ability to conduct further sensitivity analyses reduce our confidence in these estimates. While reliable data may be available at state and local levels for use in simulations of mode shift, the importance of communicating the uncertainty underlying projections to decision makers remains. Assessments of data reliability and assumptions, along with quantification of uncertainty, are necessary to enable the comparison of the risk of inaccurate results against the potential value of the estimates produced and would improve decision makers ability to reliably interpret these estimates and compare estimates across projects. In order to accomplish this and produce reliable estimates of freight diversion and uncertainty at the national level, it would be necessary to obtain complete, accurate, and valid data that are collected consistently for the model's relevant inputs.

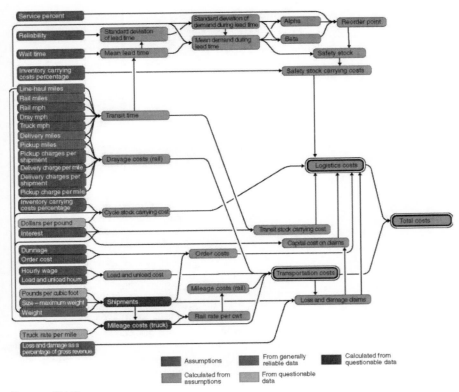

Source: GAO.

Figure 8. Intermodal Transportation and Inventory Cost (ITIC) Model Process.

Table 6. Inputs to the ITIC Model

Input	Source	Reliability	Definition
Truck rate per mile	Proprietary data	Undetermined	Per-mile cost of using a truck for shipping (2006)
Line haul miles	FRA lookup table	Reliable for our purposes	Distance traveled by truck
Pickup miles	FRA lookup table	Reliable for our purposes	Length of rail drayage at origin
Delivery miles	FRA lookup table	Reliable for our purposes	Length of rail drayage at destination
Rail miles	FRA lookup table	Reliable for our purposes	Distance traveled on rail

Table 6. (Continued)

Input	Source	Reliability	Definition
Dollars per pound	FRA commodity attribute table	Undetermined	Average value of a given commodity class
Pounds per cubic foot	FRA commodity attribute table	Undetermined	Weight per cubic foot of a given commodity class
Commodity type	Freight Analysis Framework (FAF)	Reliable for our purposes	Two-digit STGC code for commodity being carried in the shipment
Trailer size/max weight factor	FRA	Reliable for our purposes	Factor for ensuring that weight per shipment is not over legal limits or cubic footage of truck trailer or COFC
Weight	FAF	Reliable for our purposes	Total annual weight of a given commodity transported between regions (2002)
Interest	Assumption	Undetermined	Cost of capital during transit and during loss and damage claims
Inventory carrying cost %	Assumption	Undetermined	Costs associated with possession of a commodity, including capital cost, insurance, taxes, obsolescence, pilferage, transfer, handling, and storage.
Load and unload hours	Assumption	Undetermined	Amount of time needed to load or unload a truck trailer or COFC
Hourly wage	Assumption	Undetermined	Amount paid to workers loading and unloading a truck trailer or container on a flat car (COFC)
Pickup charges per shipment	Assumption	Undetermined	Flat fee charged to pick up shipments by rail
Delivery charges per shipment	Assumption	Undetermined	Flat fee charged to deliver shipments by rail
Pickup charge per mile	Assumption	Undetermined	Per-mile charge for rail drayage over 30 miles at origin
Delivery charge per mile	Assumption	Undetermined	Per-mile charge for rail drayage over 30 miles at destination
Reliability	Assumption	Undetermined	A factor used to represent the skewness of the transit time distribution for truck and rail to represent likelihood that transit time will be the predicted value

Loss and damage as a percentage of gross revenue	Assumption	Undetermined	Ratio of loss and damage costs to commodities over the gross revenue from shipping
Order cost	Assumption	Undetermined	Cost of placing an order to be shipped
Dunnage	Assumption	Undetermined	extra charge (assumed $50) to rail orders
Truck mph	Assumption	Undetermined	Average truck speed
Rail mph	Assumption	Undetermined	Average rail speed
Dray mph	Assumption	Undetermined	Average speed of drayage to/from rail
Wait time	Assumption	Undetermined	Number of days before a shipment can be transported
Service percent	Assumption	Undetermined	Probability of no stock out (inventory) during the replenishment cycle
Disaggregation	**Source**	**Reliability**	**Definition**
Origin region	FAF	Reliable for our purposes	FAF-defined regions
Destination region	FAF	Reliable for our purposes	FAF-defined regions
County establishments	QCEW	Reliable for our purposes	Proxy for the share of economic activity an individual county within a FAF region is responsible for (2006)

Source: GAO analysis of ITIC model.

Table 7. ITIC Calculations

Calculated values	Definitions
Shipments	Number of shipments per year needed to transport total annual weight
Transit time	Average amount of time (in days) from origin to destination
Mean lead time	Average amount of time in advance a shipper needs to order to receive a commodity on time
Standard deviation of lead time	Error associated with average lead time
Mean demand during lead time	Average demand (in tons) of a commodity during lead time
Standard deviation of demand during lead time	Error associated with average demand during lead time

Table 7. (Continued)

Calculated values	Definitions
Alpha	Measure of the variance of demand during lead time
Beta	Measure of the skewness of the distribution of demand during lead time
Reorder point	Amount of commodity (in tons) remaining in a shippers stock when they should reorder
Safety stock	Amount of commodity (in pounds) a shippers needs to maintain in stock to insure they won't stock out
Rail cost per one hundred pounds	Cost of transporting 100 pounds of a commodity by rail
Cycle stock carrying cost	Cost of holding inventory of a commodity
Safety stock carrying cost	Cost associated with carrying additional inventory of a commodity to prevent stock out
Capital cost on claims	Cost incurred through interest paid while filling loss and damage claims
Loss and damage claims	Cost incurred through loss and damage to commodities during transit
Order costs	Total cost (order cost plus dunnage) to place an order
In-transit stock carrying cost	Cost incurred through interest accrued while stock is in transit
Mileage costs: truck	Cost for a shipment to move from origin to destination by truck
Mileage costs: rail	Cost for a shipment to move from origin rail junction to destination rail junction
Drayage costs: rail	Cost for a shipment to move between origin/destination and rail junctions
Load and unload cost	Cost to load and unload a truck or container on a flat car
Logistics costs	Costs associated with possession of the commodity
Transportation costs	Costs associated with movement of the commodity
Total costs	Sum of transportation and logistics costs

Source: GAO analysis of ITIC model.

End Notes

[1] Data are based on a review of 439 urban areas in the United States and includes both highways and principal arterials. Yearly delay per auto commuter is the extra time spent traveling at congested speeds rather than free-flow speeds by private vehicle drivers and passengers who typically travel in peak periods. The value of travel time delay is estimated at $16 per hour of person travel and $106 per hour of truck time. Texas Transportation Institute Urban Mobility Report 2010.

[2] Forecast is based on an analysis of the Commodity Flow Survey (CFS) which is developed in partnership by the Census Bureau and the Bureau of Transportation Statistics (BTS).

[3] The primary greenhouse gasses produced by the transportation sector are carbon dioxide (CO_2), methane (CH_4), nitrous oxide (N_2O), and hydrofluorocarbon (HFC).

[4] While outside the scope of this study—the potential benefits of rail are not solely limited to emissions, congestion, and economic development benefits that result from modal shift. Improved or expanded rail service may simply increase the desire and ability of people to travel or engage in trade, and to enjoy the subsequent benefits that flow from that enhancement in mobility and access.

[5] Pub. L. No. 110-432, Div. B, 122 Stat. 4907 (October 2008).

[6] 49 U.S.C. § 26106.

[7] 49 U.S.C. § 24105.

[8] 49 U.S.C. § 24402.

[9] Pub. L. No. 111-5, Title XII, 123 Stat. 115 (2009).

[10] 74 Fed. Reg. 29900 (June 23, 2009).

[11] OMB, *Guidelines and Discount Rates for Benefit-Cost Analysis of Federal Programs*, Circular No. A-94 (Oct. 29, 1992), as revised through Dec. 8, 2009. OMB, *Principles for Federal Infrastructure Investments*, Exec. Order No. 12893 (Jan. 26, 1994). *Regulatory Analysis*, Circular No. A-4 (Sept. 17, 2003).

[12] For example, the European rail system is focused primarily on passenger operations, while the U.S. rail network is predominantly a freight transport system.

[13] As defined by revenue, for 2009, Class I railroads are freight rail carriers having annual operating revenues of $379 million or more. [49 C.F.R. 1201-1]. The railroads include CSX Transportation (CSX), BNSF Railway Company (BNSF), Union Pacific Railroad Company (Union Pacific), Norfolk Southern, Kansas City Southern Railway Company, Canadian National Railway, and Canadian Pacific Railway. Regional and short line railroads are medium-sized and small railroads, respectively, and are categorized based on operating revenues and mileage. Generally, for 2009, regional railroads are Class II railroads (carrier having annual operating revenues greater than $30 million but less than 379 million) and short line railroads are Class III railroads (carriers having annual operating revenues of $30 million or less).

[14] 49 U.S.C. § 24308.

[15] An externality is an unintended side effect (negative or positive) of an activity of one individual or firm on the well-being of others.

[16] For 2008, HFCs accounted for 3 percent, and CH_4 and N_2O together accounted for about 1.5 percent of the transportation total greenhouse gas emissions. N_2O and CH_4 gasses are released during fuel consumption, although in much smaller quantities than CO_2, and are also affected by vehicle emissions control technologies. U.S. DOT, *Transportation's Role in Reducing U.S. Greenhouse Gas Emissions*, volume 1, Synthesis Report, P. 2-5, April 2010.

[17] Data are based on "tailpipe" emissions and do not include other processes that also produce additional greenhouse gas emissions. These include the production and distribution of fuel, the manufacture of vehicles, and the construction and maintenance of transportation infrastructure. These supporting processes—known as the fuel, vehicle manufacture, and infrastructure cycles—generally are not included in U.S. transportation sector greenhouse gas estimates.

[18] GAO, *Surface Freight Transportation: A Comparison of the Costs of Road, Rail, and Waterways Freight Shipments That Are Not Passed on to Consumers*, GAO-11-134 (Washington D.C.: Jan. 26, 2011). Estimates are based on the most current data available. Estimated emissions were obtained directly from EPA and are based on the current MOVES2010 model for estimating on-road vehicle emissions. Estimates assume that nearly all on-road diesel emissions are freight-related, and 15 percent of gasoline powered vehicle emissions are freight-related.

[19] GAO, *Nextgen Air Transportation System: FAA's Metrics Can Be Used to Report on Status of Individual Programs, but Not of Overall NextGen Implementation or Outcomes*, GAO-10-629 (Washington, D.C.: July 27, 2010).

[20] Estimates are in 2010 dollars. To obtain an estimate in accident costs we included the number of fatalities multiplied by the latest value for human life used by DOT in guidance for its own analysts, and then assumed that carriers are already compensated for 50 percent of those costs. The economic costs of transportation accidents reflect the value assigned to the loss of a human life and the reduced productive life and pain and suffering related to serious injuries. (GAO-11-134).

[21] A recent legislative proposal has put forth potential policy goals for transportation that include such things as reducing delays, improving safety, reducing greenhouse gas emissions, and shifting 10 percent of freight traffic in the United States off of highways and onto other modes. See S.1036, 11th Cong. (2009).

[22] It is difficult to assess whether the benefits associated with a policy that seeks to shift traffic to rail outweigh the various costs associated with these policies. In addition, there are also costs associated with alternative approaches that may affect which one or combination of policies would be most desirable for a given situation.

[23] Pub. L. No. 110-432, Div. B, 122 Stat. 4907 (Oct. 16, 2008).

[24] In addition to these responsibilities, FRA is also responsible for developing a national rail plan. The agency also has responsibility for railroad safety oversight, providing operational and capital grants to Amtrak, and approval for Railroad Rehabilitation and Improvement Financing loans and Rail Line Relocation and Improvement Capital Grants under the Transportation Infrastructure Finance and Innovation Act (TIFIA) (see 23 U.S.C. chapter 6) and Railroad Rehabilitation and Improvement Financing (RRIF) (at 45 U.S.C. chapter 17) programs.

[25] Additional funding was provided through other FY 2009 and FY 2010 appropriations to DOT.

[26] Pub. L. No. 111-5, Title XII, 123 Stat. 115 (2009). A later, second round, known as TIGER II, was authorized and funds appropriated by the Consolidated Appropriations Act, 2010, Pub. L. No.111-117, Div. A, Title I, 123 Stat 3034, 3036 (Dec. 16, 2009).

[27] In addition to the TIGER and HSIPR programs, other DOT programs that provide investment in rail projects also consider information on project benefits and costs as part of their application processes. The TIFIA and RRIF programs allow applicants to include information on economic, environmental, and safety benefits in their applications. However, neither program provides applicants with specific requirements for assessment of potential benefits and costs.

[28] The benefits associated with policies to address external costs of transportation activities may include reductions in pollution, congestion, and improvements in safety (reducing accidents). The policies may also affect economic activity such as by increasing construction-related jobs.

[29] For the purposes of this chapter, we use the term "assessment of benefits and costs" to mean a general evaluation of benefits and costs that may encompass a variety of types of analyses and "benefit-cost analysis" refers to a formalized analysis as it is strictly defined.

[30] GAO, *Highway And Transit Investments: Options for Improving Information on Projects' Benefits and Costs and Increasing Accountability for Results*, GAO-05-172 (Washington, D.C.: Jan. 24, 2005) and GAO, *Surface Transportation: Many Factors Affect Investment Decisions*, GAO-04-744 (Washington, D.C.: June 30, 2004).

[31] See previous footnotes 24 and 27 for additional information on TIFIA and RRIF.

[32] The Federal-Aid Highway Program provides federal financial resources and technical assistance to state and local governments for constructing, preserving, and improving the National Highway System. Funding is distributed to states through annual apportionments established by statutory formulas.

[33] OMB Circular No. A-94 recognizes that "[e]stimates of benefits and costs are typically uncertain because of imprecision in both underlying data and modeling assumptions." The

type of information that would help decision makers understand the level of uncertainty associated with a benefit-cost analysis would include the key sources of uncertainty, the expected value estimates of outcomes, the sensitivity of results to important sources of uncertainty; and where possible, the probability distributions of benefits, costs, and net benefits.

[34] GAO, *Public Transportation: Improvements Are Needed to More Fully Assess Predicted Impacts of New Starts Projects,* GAO-08-844 (Washington, D.C.: July 25, 2008).

[35] More generally, infrastructure policies should be assessed with respect to benefits and costs, as per Exec. Order No. 12893 and federal guidance.

[36] GAO-11-134.

[37] According to Amtrak officials, the Northeast Corridor has experienced a 37 percent increase in ridership between Washington, D.C. and New York and 20 percent between New York and Boston over the past 10 years.

[38] A recently released report explored the relative ability of regional corridors to attract passengers based on factors that have contributed to rail ridership in other systems around the world. Petra Todorovich and Yoav Hagler, America 2050, *High Speed Rail in America,* January 2011.

[39] DOT, *National Rail Plan: Moving Forward,* Progress Report, September 2010.

[40] The Intermodal Transportation and Inventory Cost Model (ITIC) is a computer model for calculating the costs associated with shipping freight via alternative modes, namely truck and rail. The model can be used to perform policy analysis of issues concerning long-haul freight movement, such as diversion of freight shipments from truck to rail. DOT provides the ITIC model framework as a useful tool for ongoing policy studies, and shares the model, along with some internally developed data, for this purpose. We chose to use the ITIC model to simulate mode shift from truck to rail because of its federal origins and its direct applicability to freight shipments.

[41] The model has 17 default assumptions. Because of resource constraints, our analysis only varied 3 of these assumptions and considered only one change in these values, instead of varying a larger number of assumptions for a wider range of scenarios. Therefore, we cannot conclude that the model results are robust to all plausible variations in all of the model assumptions.

[42] Amtrak officials noted that dedicated high-speed rail lines make up a very small portion of worldwide rail mileage.

[43] Cited from the American Society of Mechanical Engineers in "Transportation Invest in America: Freight–Rail Bottom Line Report," American Association of State Highway and Transportation Officials (2003).

[44] Rail fuel efficiency was calculated in ton-miles per gallon to move commodity; truck fuel efficiency is calculated in lading ton-miles per gallon. Federal Railroad Administration, "Comparative Evaluation of Rail and Truck Fuel Efficiency on Competitive Corridors" (Nov. 19, 2009).

[45] Amtrak's relative fuel efficiency advantage is based on the available data in the Department of Energy's Transportation Energy Data Book http://cta.ornl.gov/data/Index.shtml, table 2.12.

[46] For example, a major rail corridor for high-value, time-sensitive container freight exists between Los Angeles and Chicago.

[47] According to Amtrak officials, intercity passenger trains also carry more passengers than the typical aircraft.

[48] Freight moved by water between 2003 and 2007 averaged only .01 fatalities per billion ton-miles. GAO has utilized ton-miles data from FHWA's Freight Analysis Framework (FAF)3 for these calculations, while the Bureau of Transportation Statistics uses a different estimate of ton-miles.

[49] Certain effects, sometimes referred to as wider economic impacts, of investments in transportation infrastructure may not be captured in standard benefit-cost analysis. These impacts may include effects related to returns to scale and agglomeration. Because markets

are often not perfect, such wider economic impacts—both positive and negative—may result from transportation investments.

[50] Other studies have shown varying potential economic impacts. For example, a study of the Trans-European Transport Network suggested that it would not change regional GDP by more than 2 percent.

[51] The European intercity passenger and freight rail systems are very different in size, structure, and scope than the U.S. rail system. For example, the European rail system is focused primarily on passenger operations, while the U.S. rail network is predominately a freight transport system. While the systems differ, the experiences of countries we visited, such as the United Kingdom and Germany provide illustrative examples of other countries experiences with policy tools that provide incentives to shift traffic to rail.

[52] We did not analyze the costs associated with trucking companies' response to the HGV policy. Therefore, we cannot determine whether the costs associated with purchasing and transitioning to a more fuel-efficient fleet outweigh the policy's environmental and other benefits, including those from the increased fuel efficiency of the trucking fleet.

[53] Allan Woodburn, "Evaluation of Rail Freight Facilities Grant Funding in Britain," School of Architecture and the Built Environment, *Transport Reviews*, 27 (3), pp. 311-326, May 2007.

[54] GAO, *High Speed Passenger Rail: Future Development Will Depend on Addressing Financial and Other Challenges and Establishing a Clear Federal Role*, GAO-09-317 (Washington, D.C.: Mar. 19, 2009).

[55] Chris Nash, "Enhancing the Cost Benefit Analysis of High Speed Rail" (paper presented at the California High Speed Rail Symposium, Berkeley, Calif., Dec. 3, 2010).

[56] We selected a nongeneralizable random sample of 20 applications from each program that included components of intercity passenger or freight rail and assessed the benefit and cost information contained in the applications based on OMB guidelines for benefit-cost analysis, with input from GAO economists and methodologists. For more information on the methodology of our study assessment, see appendix I.

[57] FRA allowed applicants to the HSIPR program to submit applications under four different funding "Tracks." The pool of HSIPR applications from which we randomly selected projects for review were from Track 2, which included applicants evaluated under PRIIA §§301 and 501, i.e., 49 U.S.C. §§ 24402 and 26106, which authorize grants to support intercity passenger rail service and development of high-speed intercity rail systems, respectively, excluding intercity passenger rail congestion projects and including only projects using Recovery Act funding. 74 Fed. Reg. 29909. Except as otherwise stated, our references to HSIPR in this portion of this chapter are to HSIPR Track 2 as defined by FRA. See appendix III for more detail.

[58] Our study assessment was limited to applications to TIGER and HSIPR that were required to include information on project benefits and costs.

[59] Of the approximately 1,450 applications DOT received for the TIGER program, DOT officials selected 166 to be forwarded to review teams for additional consideration. These applications were selected based on criteria such as project readiness and potential for job creation. The benefit and cost information contained in these 166 applications was reviewed by a team of DOT economists, who rated each evaluation for adequacy and value. For more information on these ratings, see below.

[60] Benefits and costs expected to occur in future years are discounted to account for the time value of money. In general, discounting gives relatively less weight to benefits and costs expected to occur in the future. Not discounting or using an inappropriate discount rate can affect the results of a benefit-cost analysis. OMB provides guidance on choosing appropriate discount rates for different types of investments and recommends both 3 percent and 7 percent discount rates for benefit-cost analyses of proposed investments. DOT asked applicants to the TIGER program to discount future benefits and costs using a discount rate of 7 percent and permitted them to provide an alternative analysis using a discount rate of 3 percent. However, HSIPR applicants were not required to perform benefit-cost analysis and

were not provided information on discounting in the *Federal Register* notice for the program.

[61] It is important to note that DOT did not specifically refer HSIPR applicants to this guidance. However, TIGER applicants were directed to this guidance through the federal "Notice of Funding Availability for Supplemental Discretionary Grants for Capital Investments in Surface Transportation Infrastructure" under the American Recovery and Reinvestment Act, 74 Fed. Reg. 28755 (June 17, 2009), which also directed applicants toward specific values to apply in assessing some categories of benefits.

[62] GAO-09-317.

[63] Economic research indicates that the value associated with reduction in greenhouse gas emissions can vary substantially depending on factors such as assumptions about future economic growth and discount rates.

[64] We identified TIGER applications for projects that contained rail elements. Applications included those for projects that were rail-only, as well as those that were multimodal in nature and included rail infrastructure improvements. Of these rail-related applications, DOT economists assessed the "usefulness" of benefit-cost information only for those applications that were forwarded by initial review teams for additional consideration.

[65] DOT economists grouped benefit-cost analyses submitted by TIGER applicants into four categories of usefulness: (1) very useful assessments quantified and monetized the full range of costs and benefits for which such measures are reasonably available and provided a high degree of confidence that the benefits of the project will exceed the project's costs, (2) useful assessments quantified and monetized expected benefits and costs with some gaps and provided a sufficient degree of confidence that benefits of the project will exceed the project's costs, (3) marginally useful assessments had significant gaps in their analysis of project benefits and costs and were those for which DOT was uncertain whether the benefits of the project will exceed the project's costs, and (4) nonuseful assessments did not adequately quantify and monetize benefits and costs, did not provide sufficient confidence that the benefits of the project will exceed the project's costs, and demonstrated an unreasonable absence of data and analysis.

[66] As mentioned earlier and discussed in more detail in appendix III, Track 2 applicants were selected under PRIIA §§301 and 501, i.e., 49 U.S.C. §§ 24402 and 26106, which in turn authorized grants to support intercity passenger rail capital assistance and development of high-speed intercity rail systems, respectively, using Recovery Act funding, but excluding Track 1 projects. Track 1 included Recovery Act projects authorized under PRIIA §§301 (intercity passenger rail capital assistance projects) or 302 (projects to address intercity passenger rail congestion), imposed tighter time frames, but allowed applications from a broader range of applicants, including groups of states, public rail service providers, and entities established under Interstate Compacts. 49 U.S.C. §§ 24402, 24105. 74 Fed. Reg. 29900, 29908-29917.

[67] DOT announced the availability of $600 million in federal discretionary grant funding for transportation projects through the TIGER II program in June 2010 and announced TIGER II recipients in October 2010.

[68] Notice of Funding Availability for the Department of Transportation's National Infrastructure Investments Under the Transportation, Housing and Urban Development, and Related Agencies Appropriations Act for 2010, 75 Fed. Reg. 30460 (June 1, 2010).

[69] Life-cycle cost analysis can be used for the consideration of certain transportation investment decisions. In life-cycle cost analysis, all the relevant costs that occur throughout the life of a proposed project, not just the originating expenditures, are included. Costs accounted for in life-cycle cost analysis include the effects of construction and maintenance activities on users.

[70] This is a data set maintained by the Federal Highway Administration (FHWA) that estimates commodity flows and related freight transportation activity among states, sub-state regions, and major international gateways. See http://ops.fhwa.dot.gov/freight/freight_analysis/faf/

index.htm . FAF uses data from the Commodity Flow Survey, a nationally representative survey of freight shipments administered by the Bureau of Transportation Statistics (BTS). See http://www.bts.gov/publications/commodity_flow_survey/index.html .

[71] U.S. Department of Transportation, Federal Railroad Administration, *ITIC-IM Version 1.0: Intermodal Transportation and Inventory Cost Model Highway-to-Rail Intermodal User's Manual*, March 2005.

[72] Approximately 34,000 kilometers of Germany's rail infrastructure are managed by Deutsche Bahn's DB Netz, while an additional 4,000 kilometers are run by other infrastructure managers.

[73] HGV toll revenue may also be used to maintain and upgrade the rail and waterway networks.

[74] American Recovery and Reinvestment Act of 2009, Pub. L. No. 111-5, Title XII, 123 Stat. 115 (2009) (Recovery Act).

[75] Pub. L. No. 110-432, Div.B, 122 Stat. 4907 (October 2008).

[76] 74 Fed. Reg. 29900 (June 23, 2009).

[77] Consolidated Appropriations Act, 2010, Pub. L. 111-117, Div. A, Title I, 123 Stat 3034, 3056 (Dec.16, 2009).

[78] Tracks 1 and 2 of the HSIPR program were funded from an $8 billion appropriation of Recovery Act funds, while tracks 3 and 4 of the HSIPR program were funded from an appropriation of approximately $90 million from FY 2008 and FY 2009 Capital Grants to States-Intercity Passenger Service DOT appropriations. Each track prioritized evaluation criteria differently.

[79] Pub. L. No. 111-5, Title XII, 123 Stat. 115 (2009).

[80] 74 Fed. Reg. 28755 (June 17, 2009).

[81] Consolidated Appropriations Act, 2010, Pub. L. 111-117, Div. A. Title I, 123 Stat 3034 (Dec. 16, 2009).

[82] Applicants requesting less than $20 million in federal funding were not required to submit a benefit-cost analysis for proposed projects, while those requesting between $20 million and $100 million in federal funding were required to include a basic benefit-cost analysis, and those requesting greater than $100 million were required to submit a more comprehensive benefit-cost analysis.

[83] The ITIC model was first developed in 1995 under a joint effort by the U.S. Department of Transportation Office of the Secretary (OST), the Federal Railroad Administration (FRA), the Federal Highway Administration (FHWA) and the Bureau of Transportation Statistics (BTS). Since 1995, DOT has modified and updated the model, and used it in DOT's *Comprehensive Truck Size and Weight Study*, which was submitted to Congress in 2000.

[84] The ITIC model is one tool of many that are available to aid in analysis, and its results should not be considered as the sole answer when making decisions or advancing a policy position. It should be used in concert with other models to build a framework for decision making.

[85] Our choices of data sources were similar to data used in previous applications of the ITIC model by FRA and FHWA, but we selected more recent data when possible. We did not assess whether sufficiently reliable data were available at more disaggregate scales, such as single traffic corridors, individual states, or within regions.

[86] GA O, *Applied Research and Methods: Assessing the Reliability of Computer-Processed Data*, GAO-09-680G (Washington D.C.: July 2009).

[87] Specifically, partial data was available for truck rates, the weight per cubic foot, and the value per pound of particular commodities.

[88] Reliability factor describes the shape of the reliability distribution, rather than a direct measure of truck reliability.

INDEX

D

E

F

G

H

I